Message from Scientific Anglers

ding for Bass.") After printing over 2 million copies of the *Handbooks* and trying to explain to our eager readers why we only published them once a year, we launched the Scientific Anglers *Fly Fishing Quarterly* and offered subscriptions.

Along the way, we discovered the learning power of video. We found ways to take things that were nearly impossible to understand when you read about them in a book and used video to make them easy to learn. The camera, acting as an educated eye, focuses the viewer on what is essential about a subject. We know that being able to visualize an idea or a skill is a very important part of learning and that nothing does it better than video. Now, after producing 18 fly fishing videos with more on the way, you can see the masters of the sport explain their strategies for hooking fish and watch them demonstrate how it's all done. Just like being at their shoulder. No more guessing for you!

By now, Scientific Anglers number one priority must be obvious to you: helping fly fishers like yourself become more successful and increase your enjoyment. It is our company's mission. Quite simply, we want to remove as much of the confusion and mystery from this sport, but none of the magic that makes it so wonderful.

"OK," you say, "that's great. But what's in it for SA?" The answer is very basic. Fly fishing is our only business at Scientific Anglers and we've long since become the world's largest producers of fly lines. But we know if we can't help anglers like you expand your involvement in fly fishing and if we can't bring new generations of anglers into the sport, we can't grow. And, without growth, we can't survive in today's competitive economy. So we've intensified our effort even more.

The *Guidebook*, our first softbound book, is the latest form of our obsession with providing helpful information. Why a book? Aren't there enough good books? In fact, isn't there plenty of good information about fly fishing available today? Yes, without a doubt. But something seems to be missing. Anglers who read all these magazines, books and videos, need a structure where they can hang the bits and

pieces of advice they pick up. They need a thought process that will enable them to break the code behind any angling situation they face.

This *Guidebook* will prevent you from getting lost in the magnitude of information available. When things start to get confusing, all the information, key relationships and guiding principles that are the foundation of the sport are here, ready for your review.

In fact, I suggest frequent re-reading because, like the SA Bass Bulletin I stumbled on, the content of this book is principle-driven. So, as your expertise and experience grows, the very same principles you read only months earlier will take on additional meaning. The How, When and, most importantly, the Why become even more clear, giving you the power to solve ever more complex angling riddles.

If you have only started to sample the joys of fly fishing, I deeply envy you. There has never been a better time to be a fly fisher. The learning curve has been dramatically shortened because the excess luggage of myth and mystery has been eliminated. There are dozens of excellent fly fishing schools across the country, even a few pioneer efforts in saltwater, to help you over the hurdles and hundreds of top quality fly shops that can help you sort through the specialized, high performance fly tackle that will complement your skills.

To keep you growing, there is a wonderful array of fly fishing magazines and, for those who are always saying, "I just don't have the time," there is the ultimate time-saver and learning accelerator, the instructional videotape. Given the available tools, I am confident you can easily learn in one year what it took me a whole decade to sort out. In a few quick years, you may even have it mastered.

When you do, all I ask is that you empathize with the poor old duffers you'll encounter, still struggling to crack the riddle of the day long after you've had your fun. Stop and give them a hand. You see, one of them could be me. Enjoy.

Howard West

Howard West
Scientific Anglers Project Manager

***Tarpon released
unharmed, angler booked
for life!***

Table of Contents

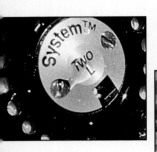

Overview

For over 25 years, our mission at Scientific Anglers has been to help avid anglers like you become more successful fly fishers and increase your level of enjoyment of the sport. We do this by "removing the mystery and none of the magic." Through years of research and personal experience, our people in the laboratories and in the field have helped us develop our Formula for Success so that all anglers can learn about fly fishing in the fastest way possible and enjoy all the sport has to offer.

And, now, we've written the *Guidebook to Fly Fishing Mastery* so we can share this important information with all interested fly fishers everywhere. This book isn't for the beginner (we have a book called *Fly Fishing Made Easy* for them). It's for those anglers who've been fly fishing for some time, but want to become more success-ful—as good as they can be.

We start with a description of the "Formula for Success" that can accelerate your learning and eliminate the frustrations that come from acquiring new skills. You'll see the whole experience of fly fishing—not just bits and pieces—and learn to answer the "Why" behind the many challenging situations you'll find in the field.

Then we move into the main part of the *Guidebook*: "Foundations of Fly Fishing Mastery." In this chapter, you'll learn how to more effectively locate your favorite species and choose the best equipment you'll need to catch them. This section will change the way you look at fly fishing as you begin to see with expert eyes. Then, you'll discover the different ways your equipment can help you present your flies that will dramatically improve your level of success. You'll know what you need to do to develop your casting skills so you can take fish in all situations and conditions. We'll also give you suggestions on ways to improve your chances of angling success through preparation before you get into the field.

The final chapter, "Solving the Riddle," features master anglers who tell you how they use the Formula for Success to solve the riddle of a challenging angling problem. These personal experiences will help you better understand the knowledge of the "Foundations" chapter and show you how to apply these concepts to your own angling experiences.

Certainly this approach isn't the only way nor is it the way for everyone. One of the great things about fly fishing is that it can be as simple or complex as you want to make it. Each individual decides what's fun about the sport and can change their mind any time they want. That's one nice thing about the SA approach to fly fishing mastery: you can set your own itinerary and make many stops along the way.

And you will find each stage of the journey can lead to equally fascinating side trips. Maybe, you'll become fascinated with entomology and want to learn everything you can about bugs trout eat, then learn to tie flies to imitate them. Some people collect fly rods, others love to build their own. An interest in saltwater fishing and its fascinating environment can give you op-portunities to explore many exotic places. And these are only some of the possibilities.

Whatever you decide about the role of fly fishing in your life, you will discover it is truly a lifetime sport and it can become a joyful, satisfying part of your life whenever you decide to begin. During its long history, people have enjoyed fly fishing because of the richness and variety of experience that is at the heart of the angling life. And, for those who choose to make fly fishing part of their life today, there has never been a time in its 1500 year history that the sport has so much to offer, so many possibilities. Best of all, it has never been easier to master. With the enormous amount of information gathered—particularly in the last 10 years—now available in books, articles and the powerful new medium of video, an angler with basic physical skills can be fishing at intermediate to advanced levels within in year!

The Formula for Success

You've been fly fishing now for some time. You've put lots of time and energy into this sport and there's no doubt in your mind this is something you want to pursue in the years ahead. But there is some doubt about the kind of

There were those times when little went right and they made you wonder.

Howard West

success you've had so far.

With the help of a local fishing tackle dealer or a good friend, you've picked up a lot of new ideas and techniques. All that time learning the basic knots and casting, the time you spent reading up on how fish feed and where they hold. It's paid off. When things were right, you've had some spectacular days on the water. You could do no wrong. Nature's mysteries were revealed and you solved the riddle! These were the best of times, times to be cherished.

But there were those times when little went right and they made you wonder: do I really know enough, am I skillful enough to enjoy the kind of success that some others seem to have? Am I learning fast enough?

These days are not forgotten either. Times when the bass didn't cooperate in a usually productive lily pad cove and you fished the water for endless hours with no strikes. Or, at the end of a long day's wait on the flats, fish moved in quickly and your cast fell short, out of range—the one great chance at a monster bonefish lost forever.

The Science Behind the Art

Window Peeking

by Mary Dry

Some people feel they have to learn everything there is to know about insects, lines, reels, hatches, streambeds and fly patterns just to catch a few lousy fish! What a hassle. I had a better solution: Tag along with a knowledgeable fishing partner on lots of fishing trips and, when the going gets tough, shake him down for answers—that's the real Formula for Success!

So there we were, my trusty fishing partner, Mike, and I, on Silver Creek in midsummer. We'd driven over from a nearby campground around 7:30 to fish the evening rise and, much to our delight, the rainbows were on tiny mayflies ("baetis," Mike said). The fishing was typical for Silver. Endless downstream floats of tiny imitations over huge fish that bulged and swirled on the rafts of naturals that covered the water. The tiny flies were everywhere. In my nose, my hair, all over my clothes—even my waders were covered with eggs the flies had dropped in the water! After two fishless hours, though, my enthusiasm was fading with the light. The back of my neck hurt and the water was ungodly cold.

The hatch was dying out, for sure, but there were plenty of rises below us. I watched for awhile and laughed as Mike would drift his fly unscathed through a pod of fish and mutter, "Cowards! Dirty rotten cowards!" No one else was catching fish either, so I didn't really mind. One by one, the other anglers moved out of the water and headed for their cars. Still, I could see Mike wasn't about to leave when fish were still visible—right *there*, damn it—and we couldn't catch them.

(continued on page 6)

Maybe it was that time, during a blizzard caddis hatch, when the trout fed in a frenzy and they wouldn't take your dry fly. Slashes, yes. But no fish. And the guy who fished downstream from you—the one who had a fish on every time you looked up—who said later at the car, "God. What a night! They really smashed my pupa imitation. Fished it just under the surface."

On days like this, you only come away with a nagging question, "Why?"

But, for those who truly come to enjoy the art of fly fishing, this question lies at the heart of the matter. Because trying to answer the "Why's" of this fascinating sport gives us our highest Highs and lowest Lows! Our greatest thrills come from cracking the most complicated codes, the toughest riddles we encounter in our angling. Yet, it is this same complexity that can create so much frustration over the inability to succeed in different situations. Just when you think you have things figured out, they change!

Angling Success

Not a mathematical formula, our Formula for Success is a thought process that will teach you the right questions to ask to help you solve the riddle of any angling situation you encounter.

We've always been intrigued by the fact that 10 percent of the anglers catch 90 percent of the fish. Through the years, we've studied the reasons for this catch ratio and discovered that the best anglers have their own formula for success. Based on what they told us and our own research, we developed a formula that works for us:

Success = Location + Presentation + Preparation

The implications of this formula—which applies to all types of fishing—are simple: it will help you take more and bigger fish in the shortest time possible. But, like the famous formula, $E=MC^2$, its simplicity is only on the surface. Supporting this formula is a vast amount of information

It will help you take more fish and bigger fish in the shortest time possible.

Window Peeking, cont.

Then, suddenly, before I could ask Mike. "What other pattern I should try?" I spotted them. Caddis. Big dark brown ones, barely visible in the black shadows on my left, dancing up against the bank. For the first time since I had started fly fishing trout, it occurred to me that maybe I had been wrong about my approach to this whole thing. Maybe my trusty partner didn't always have the answer. Maybe he couldn't always see what was really going on. I could plainly see caddis on the water and, maybe, that's what the trout were looking at through their window.

I quickly tied a caddis emerger (#16 seemed about the right size) onto my long leader. No weight. I figured a soggy fly would get below the surface in these gentle currents just fine. At first I continued casting downstream slightly to my left with a little mend, thinking that would give the fly time to sink. No luck. Then something from my first-ever fishing trip came to mind. If I cast across the stream toward the bank on my left where the current ran stronger, then let the fly drift down, sinking and swinging in to the main channel, it would rise up to the surface at the end of the drift. Just like a real caddis emerger.

On the first cast, I watched the fly in my mind's eye as it sank close to the bank, then swung into the current. Just as I could see it moving to the surface, I felt a strong take and a fish was on! Instinctively, I glanced to my right at Mike who was intently floating some new baetis pattern

over his pod of fish. I hadn't told him about my new idea and, now that it had worked, I wanted to alert him to the miracle taking place right beside him. But no sound came out.

Finally, I gasped out something that sounded like, "I...I, uh got one."

"What?" he asked without taking his eyes from his fly.

My fish sprang to the surface. Yes, it really was true. Mike turned to watch as I played the fish on this wonderful river. The fish tried all the usual tricks, but I kept the pressure on the 7X tippet. And then the fish was in my hands.

"Look, look," I said. My heart was pounding. But, somehow, I got the hook out and held the beautiful rainbow a few seconds, admiring its colors as they glowed in the moon that had sneaked up on us. I let it glide back into the icy water.

I told Mike about the caddis I saw. And how I had used the emerger pattern to take the fish. He tied on one of his own and moved back to his spot. We both fished there side by side on Silver Creek all alone in the moonlight.

But I couldn't get that fish out of my mind. It was remarkable. Somehow, I'd absorbed enough information along the way to hook a fish on my own without expert advice. And that fish. Well, I used to laugh at people who can remember the precise circumstances of every fish they've caught (like Jack Nicklaus remembers every hole of golf he ever played).

But that fish I will remember always.

and many techniques that will open new and exciting pathways to fly fishing success. Our formula won't change the world, but it should change the way you think about a portion of the world. If we can do this, we've accomplished our goal.

🎣 *Formula for Success: Trout*
Three of fly fishing's experts, Gary Borger, Doug Swisher and Rick Haefle, teach you how to consistently catch more trout and bigger trout even under the most difficult conditions.

They'll show you how to use the Scientific Anglers Formula for Success to locate trout, to identify what they're feeding on and how to best imitate that food.

This is the tape that will take you beyond the basics of the Formula for Success and show you how to apply the formula to fishing for trout. By focusing on one species, you'll begin to build a base of special knowledge that's needed to have consistent angling success when fishing for trout.

Location: *Learn "where, why and when" fish will be in a specific place*

It means understanding your quarry—whatever species you choose—so you'll know why the fish behave the way they do. Where they find the food they eat. What kind of shelter they are likely to seek. What effect temperature has on their feeding activity. This kind of knowledge will tell you the most likely places fish will hold in any body of water within the daily and seasonal rhythms of their life. And knowing where fish are located will increase your angling productivity tremendously because you'll be putting your fly in the 10 percent of the water where fish are holding.

Once you understand fish behavior and can locate them, you must be able to present your fly naturally at their feeding level.

Presentation: *Learn to choose the right equipment for specific situations and conditions and use it to get your fly in front of the fish in a natural manner*

Guiding Principle: You must learn to control the drift or retrieve of your fly line because it, in turn, controls the movement of your fly. Where the fly line goes, the fly follows.

This starts with very thorough knowledge of your equipment. How a complete understanding of your equipment—its effective range and limitations—will help you select the right equipment for whatever challenge you face. How balanced fly fishing systems and the proper casting techniques will help you cast your fly with a new kind of power, accuracy and just pure casting pleasure. And, most importantly, it means knowing how to use your equipment so you can put your fly where you want it under any conditions, especially in the wind.

The simple fact is that the best fly casters catch the biggest fish. Why? Because they can consistently put their fly in the most difficult locations, the places where the best fish are. And, once they get their fly to the strike zone, they know how to keep it there longer, increasing their chances of a take. How do they do this? They understand the whole concept of presentation: mending line on the water and in the air, feeding slack line and, at the core of all presentation, the subtleties of casting that give them complete control in any situation.

Once you start using the Formula for Success to organize your thinking, it will totally change your fishing experience. You won't get lost any more. When you're on new water, things will look very familiar and you'll start feeling more comfortable. And, when you start using new presentation methods, you will not believe the kind of success you'll have and the super Highs this brings!

But the key to making the Formula work is thorough preparation.

Preparation: *Learn the things you need to do before you get on the water to increase your angling pleasure and your chances of angling success*

Fishing is truly the great equalizer. The fish don't care who you are, how much money you make or what equipment you have. To catch them, you'll need knowledge and skill. Ten thousand dollars worth of tackle won't get the job done if you can't

Three Objectives of Presentation:

Accuracy: Hit a specific target with your fly.

Feeding level/ depth: Put your fly in the strike zone

Natural drag-free drift (dry fly or nymph) and natural retrieve (sub-surface fly): Cause the fish to take.

cast effectively. A thousand dollars worth of flies won't catch a single fish if your fly isn't properly presented to the fish. You must learn these principles, strategies and skills yourself. No one else can do it for you.

A great person once said, "The harder I work, the luckier I get!" And you'll find this is true for your angling skills as well. This includes understanding the major concepts of fly fishing and, of critical importance, practicing your presentation techniques. The successes your preparation will bring will only increase the excitement of preparing for your next outing.

And, once you have acquired the knowledge and developed the skills for success, there is also a very subtle side to all of this. The psychology of success or the emotional side of the angling experience. It may be dealing with a moment so exciting that you cannot function effectively— mentally or physically—in a given situation. A sudden feeding frenzy will do this to almost any angler! Your heart is pounding. The breath quickens. You can't think straight, let alone cast! Or, perhaps the toughest test you may find yourself doing what you know is right and not taking fish. Challenges like these do not disappear with experience. To handle them requires a mental toughness you can develop if you

will use the Formula for Success for all the angling situations you face.

This kind of knowledge and skill also brings the thrill of hooking lots of fish— particularly bigger fish—and we'll make sure you know how to land and release them, even tarpon, the ultimate saltwater thrill!

We would be the first to agree: this is not the only way nor is it the way for everyone. But we have watched this angling approach bring the greatest angling pleasure to those who make the commitment to learn these principles and skills. And, for some who choose to follow this path to its end, they will discover the ultimate destination, fly fishing mastery, the ability to solve the riddle in any angling situation.

A look ahead

The rest of our book will explain what you need to know to develop your fly fishing talents.

In the following chapter, "The Foundations of Fly Fishing," you'll learn the essential concepts and techniques of fly fishing. The guiding principles we discuss will enable you to understand the "Why" behind the angling choices you make and help you build a base of knowledge critical to your development as an angler. Knowing these principles is the only way to understand the "How, Where and Why" of angling.

After the "Foundation" chapter comes "Solving the Riddle" where you'll learn how fly fishing masters use the presentation part of the Formula. The way they apply fly fishing theory to real angling situations will help you better understand these concepts and show you how to apply them to your own angling experience.

Will Breuster

Faced with heavy current in this run, the angler must sink his fly deep to hook fish.

Catch & Release

*I*n the Good Old Days, when there were few fishers and an abudance of quality water, it was very common to kill huge "limits" of fish everywhere. The historical photos taken from the mountain waters of Yellowstone Park to the saltwater deep of the Keys testify to this practice that drew strength from the days of subsistence harvesting of wild game.

But, soon after the middle of this century, a problem emerged. The growing popularity of all kinds of fishing and the diminishing quality of lakes, rivers and oceans of the world combined to seriously reduce the numbers of native fishes. The first defense came from state fisheries people who decided to shrink the limits of fish. This helped some, but did not reduce the effects of fishing pressure on popular waters.

Another response was the "put-and-take" strategy that still drives the massive hatchery programs thriving in virtually every state. This view attempts to solve the problem of keeping fish in a world that can no longer supply enough to satisfy anglers and still retain self-supporting populations of fish.

But, soon after the limitations of these efforts became apparent, a new ethic emerged to guide the actions of anglers everywhere: "Catch-and-Release."

Ever since Lee Wulff's rallying cry, "A trout is too valuable a resource to catch only once," we have seen a growing support across this country and many other places around the world for catch-and-release fishing. The ever-increasing numbers of anglers for all species has only made this idea more relevant than ever before.

It's advantages are compelling. By safely releasing the fish we catch, we permit the natural selection process to do its job to the benefit of species and anglers alike. By letting the Big Ones get away, we permit the genes of the most successful adaptors to the environment and the biggest fish replenish the gene pool of the species. Numbers of fish are controlled by the limits of the environment as they always have before anglers who killed fish upset the natural balance. Successful catch-and-release programs can in time eliminate the need for put-and-take fish and support what is left of already damaged wild fisheries.

For a variety of reasons, the support of this ethic comes from many sources and its success is reflected in many ways. Scientific Anglers was an early voice that lobbied actively for catch-and-realease and started a trophy release club in the early '70's. B.A.S.S. fishing tournaments, which have become so popular in recent years, now require catch-and-release of all fish, a highly visible gesture that has had great impact on non-professional anglers. Many resorts across the world now insist their guests follow some type of catch-and-release program when fishing on their waters. Many states have developed special regulated waters that are exclusively flies-only, catch-and-release water for trout. Fish managers who study the impact of such programs report resounding success in a very short period of time. More and bigger fish is the standard result.

So, regardless of the value you place on your favorite species, we encourage your support of catch-and-release in whatever way you can. Learn the proper techniques for releasing fish to increase chances of mortality. Voluntarily release your catch—particularly those "fish of a lifetime" that beg to be mounted—even if you fish unregulated waters. (To preserve your angling success, take photos or have the fiberglass mounts made from those photos as alternative to killing a fish for the wall.) Support fishing organizations and their legislative efforts. In these ways, we can continue the spread of this powerful ethic than can only improve the quality of fishing and maintain this resource for the future.

*F*or those who choose to follow this path to its end, they will discover the ultimate destination, fly fishing mastery

Foundations of Fly Fishing

The Cornerstone for Success

*L*ike so many journeys, the first step to fly fishing success is having a clear picture of your destination. That's what we looked at in the preceding chapter, "Formula for Success." Now, the next step, is to examine the way to reach that destination.

The key to fly fishing mastery is seeing with expert eyes.

Do you remember the first time you looked at a piece of water you wanted to fish? Maybe it was a beautiful mountain stream. Or maybe it was a huge lake a friend said was "full of bass." The water looked like a blank sheet of paper. Right? But, in time, you began to see some differences that were important keys to likely places fish were. Perhaps, then, you began to look beneath the surface for a glimpse into the world of your favorite species. What kinds of foods it ate. The prime feeding times. Likely hiding spots. This all helped improve your angling success, particularly when they weren't feeding on top.

The Trout and the Fly

Brian Clark and John Goddard's discussions of the trout's visual perception of its environment, how it reacts to what it sees and what images created by a trout fly will produce a strike. Includes a series of new fly patterns designed for difficult trout, how to locate trout—particularly, by sight—and a comprehensive analysis of rise forms that will help in fly selection. A very unique, original book with hundreds of underwater photographs that will let you look through the trout's window and change the way you look at the world.

Do you remember the first time you looked at a fly rod? Maybe it was with a friend on a local pond or in your favorite tackle shop. The rod looked very long and felt funny when you waggled it. Real soft and springy. After you tried fly fishing with your own tackle and other friends' outfits, you began to see some important differences in fly rods. The bigger, stiffer rods that cast a heavier line were much easier to use when you fished big flies, especially in windy conditions. The lighter, more flexible rods were great for casting small flies to small fish and made playing them lots of fun. You began to understand how individual rods were designed for different kinds of fishing and how they made the fishing more enjoyable.

Just because they're easy to locate doesn't mean they're easy to fool.

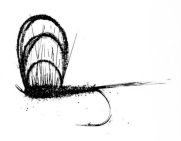

A thorough understanding of how to locate your favorite species and to choose the equipment you'll need to get your fly to these fish—wherever they are—will certainly change the way you look at fly fishing forever. And, more importantly, seeing with expert eyes will bring you angling success beyond anything you might imagine.

But this is only a part of the Formula for Success.

We're also going to explain the many different ways your equipment can help you present your flies to fish you've located in ways that will sometimes mean the difference between catching and not catching fish, maybe the fish of a lifetime. You'll develop your casting skills to a high level so you can present the fly to fish with the accuracy and control needed to take fish consistently in all conditions and situations.

The learning itself is an exciting process.

Understanding the species you pursue in new ways—where these fish are likely to be, the behavior of the foods they eat and how they react to temperature—may become one of the more interesting and enjoyable things you like about the sport. Then there's the casting. You'll be amazed at what you can do with a rod and line with some sound instruction. You'll really enjoy making different casts and you'll find yourself practicing just for the pure fun of it. And, one day, when you double-haul your fly way out there in a strong headwind and take a fish you would have ordinarily passed up because you couldn't get your fly out that far, you'll get a special thrill that goes beyond just hooking and landing another fish!

Like any learning process, your pursuit of fly fishing knowledge and skill will change you over time. You'll feel more confident when you face tough angling problems because more and more you'll find you have the ability to solve the riddles on your own. Your increasing successes on the water will only strengthen that confidence. You'll notice that you are taking

Seeing with expert eyes will bring you angling success beyond anything you might imagine.

Here are the three basic water types found in moving water: Riffle, Run and Flat (these illustrations are taken from the hardbound guidebook that comes with the Anatomy of a Trout Stream videotape in the Mastery Learning System series.)

more fish and bigger fish than other anglers who share the water with you. Or, you may be the only angler taking any fish at all. More and more frequently, other fly fishers will ask your advice about the fishing or seek bits of key information to help them solve a problem. One day, it will become very apparent that what you see is very different than what other anglers see. That's because you are now seeing with expert eyes.

Locating Fish—Freshwater

No amount of fly casting talent or choice of flies will help the fly fisher who cannot find fish when they are feeding below the surface! To put this matter in perspective, consider the 90/10 Rule: fish will feed at least 90 percent of the time below the surface and will occupy only 10 percent of the water you fish.

The key to locating fish depends on your ability to find where a fish's needs are being met in a dynamic, changing environment. This is no easy task since those needs can change dramatically from day to day or even minute to minute. The baitfish that caused a feeding frenzy in the shallows may come and go within minutes. Or trout feeding in a pool may suddenly stop taking nymphs deep and begin feeding on emergers in the surface film.

So, to find the species you pursue, you must understand how the fish survives in its environment and, like the experts, you'll need to look at the world from the fish's perspective.

Fish Behavior

The behavior of all species on this planet is driven by a need to survive in a tough, hostile environment.

Dynamic forces in nature keep a fish's life in a constant state of flux. Within the larger rhythms of the seasons and the fish's life cycle, there are the variables such as food supply, temperature and oxygen plus the ever-present danger from predators of all shapes and sizes, including man.

These forces are constants in the lives of whatever species you pursue and, to locate fish consistently in still or moving water, you must develop a sure sense of how fish behave. And this is an individual matter. The comfort range of water temperature, for example, is very different for brown, rainbow and brook trout. Water that will hold active, feeding browns may be too warm for brookies. Seasonal changes that influence water temperature a few degrees can clear the shallows of a particular species like tarpon and can mean the difference between fish and no fish at all.

Anatomy of a Trout Stream

Aquatic biologist and author, Rick Haefle, shows you how to read the water and how to respond as conditions change. Learn to dissect a stream from end to end. Understand the basic needs of the trout and where to find them. Recognize the important food in all types of water. Become adept at

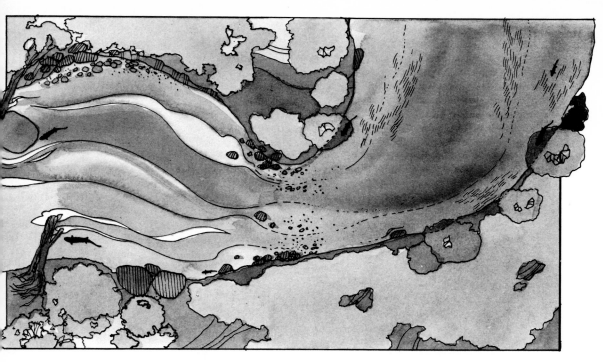

selecting the proper fly and presenting it to imitate the natural's behavior. With this knowledge, you can plan your strategy to fish any piece of water and consistently catch more and bigger trout.

Reading the Water

Because fish feed on top for such a short period (if at all) each day, anglers need to determine where fish are feeding below the surface. This skill of "reading the water" is actually the ability to create a clear picture of the fish's world beneath the surface.

When creating such pictures, remember: the surface of moving water is a mirror of the bottom, while the surface of still water is a window to the bottom.

Moving Water

When fishing moving water, regardless of species, the best way to approach the problem of locating fish is to isolate the four basic water types: riffle, run, pool and flat. Because of the individual characteristics of each water type, fish will react differently to the natural forces that influence their behavior. For example, when nymphs become active in the riffles, trout will often leave the protection of deeper water and move into the shallow water to feed. As you analyze the section of stream you plan to fish, you should also keep in mind one other important thing: fish are usually holding in fixed locations near some type of structure that protects them from predators

and energy-draining currents.

• Riffles—This is shallow water (a few inches to a few feet deep) with a rocky bottom and a fast current, forcing fish to make quick decisions about your fly. Though fish are not usually as selective here, the shallow depths narrow the fish's cone of vision and require a fly be placed right over them. This is an excellent location for trout during hot spells because of good oxygen and temperature levels in broken water. It is also a great place for food because sunlight reaches the bottom, nourishing plants important to aquatic foods that fish and their food sources feed on.

•Runs—Usually located between a riffle and a pool, this is deeper water (three to six feet) than a riffle with a smoother, less choppy surface. Fish move into runs to rest, often holding in front of boulders. Look for them at the head (below riffle) because food dumps in here, in current seams (fast/slow water meet on top or bottom) and along banks and overhanging vegetation (terrestrials).

Fish have a wider cone of vision here in the deeper water, enabling them to see anglers better and making them less vulnerable to predators. You will need longer casts and a more cautious approach. Also, different insects live here because of less sunlight (fewer plants).

• Pools—Often below a run, this slow water sanctuary usually holds the biggest fish in the river because it best meets all the

Think of the cone of vision as the "window" out of which trout view their surroundings.

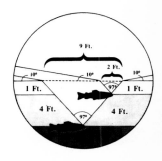

fish's needs. Fish holding here have lots of time to inspect your fly and, typically, find less diversity of insects but bigger food sources like baitfish and crustaceans. The large cone of vision demands extreme caution in stalking, while the depth makes it difficult to spot fish. During hot weather periods, pools are good places to look for fish because the deeper the water, the cooler the temperature.

Look for the three distinct parts of a pool's structure:

Head—Food washes in from riffle or run and gets concentrated here, often on a lip or drop off.

Body—Fish often cruise these slow, deep currents.

Tailout—Rocky, shallow shelf that resembles a flat.

Flats—Shallow but smooth water surface which creates a small cone of vision when fish feed on top and makes close approaching less difficult. Only real protection is weeds and overhanging vegetation which, along with the sunlight, create a tremendous food factory.

Stillwater

When fishing stillwaters, the problem of finding fish is more complicated because the location keys are not so obvious from the water surface. But you can break stillwater into three basic areas that have very specific qualities that influence fish behavior. You can also look for many differ-

ent types of physical features of the water that will attract fish in stillwaters, which like fish in moving water, need shelter. But, unlike fish in moving water who wait for the food the currents bring them, fish in still waters must be on the move if they are to survive.

In most general terms, you can divide a lake, pond or reservoir into three parts by water depth:

• The bottom layer is comprised of silt, decayed vegetation and various structures. Often a location for fish seeking protection from predators or high temperatures.

• The shoreline is the most important angling portion of stillwater, extending from the edge of the vegetation to the shore. This is a hotbed of plant and aquatic life that provides the major food sources.

• The transition layer is found between the edge of the vegetation and the top of the coldest water. Fish will sometimes suspend in this layer, moving back and forth between the shoreline and bottom layer.

But the real task of locating fish in stillwaters begins with identifying key physical features that will attract fish. And, as you analyze the water, it's best to make notes on a map you buy or draw yourself. It may take time away from your fishing and some effort on your part—chatting up local anglers or conservation staff, hiking to

Anatomy of stillwater: bottom layer, shoreline and transition layer.

higher elevations for better observation and methodical scouting of the water with both eyes wide open—to get an accurate picture of the water you want to fish. But, in the end, all your preparation will pay off in more productive time on the water.

Big Water

With practice and patience, anglers do just fine identifying these same kinds of structures when locating fish on smaller, more intimate waters. But, when you move onto larger waters, you'll probably be looking through the eyes of a beginner. The way to adjust your vision to bigger water is to break it into several pieces of smaller water and look at them separately. Like so many of these fly fishing skills, it will take time, but you will soon be comfortable reading any water you choose to fish, regardless of size.

Lake Fishing With a Fly
Written by leading stillwater experts, Randall Kaufmann and Ron Cordes, this is the most comprehensive book available on fly fishing in lakes. You'll learn how to locate fish, their main food sources and the best ways to present believeable imitations of the available food sources.

Next, let's look at the other key factor in locating fish: the foods they eat.

Food

To be successful locating fish, you need to know not only where fish feed but also what they eat. And, once again, there is far more here than meets the eye at first glance.

If you look at a body of water through expert eyes, you will see a relatively complex food chain that ranges from tiny, microscopic plants to large, powerful animals. The species you pursue will be somewhere along that food chain and, to fully understand that species' behavior, you will need to look at its life in this complex, dynamic environment.

For example, during the summer runs of Alaskan salmon, millions of fish will leave the ocean and return to spawn in the rivers of their birth. As the salmon lay their eggs, rainbow trout, arctic char and grayling will feed on those eggs, while great Alaskan brown bears will feed on the dying salmon. The millions of salmon the bears don't eat will fertilize the stream bottom for the next generation of salmon who start the Great Cycle over again. An egg fly pattern drifted along the bottom of spawning waters will attract numerous species of fish. All these species are in one place at the same time because each of their needs is best met there. The more you understand of this dynamic interaction between the closest links in the food chain to the species you're fishing for, the more success-

The real task of locating fish in stillwaters begins with identifying key physical features that will attract fish.

15

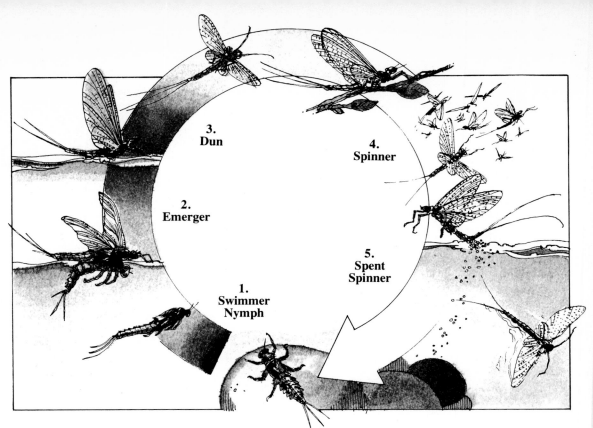

3.
Dun

2.
Emerger

4.
Spinner

5.
Spent
Spinner

1.
Swimmer
Nymph

Lifecycle of a mayfly.

ful you'll be in locating them and determining what they're feeding on.

This process can range from the very complex—determining what stage of a specific insect's life the fish are feeding on—to the very simple—identifying some common baitfish in the shallows. If trout are your passion, for example, understanding the life cycles and behavior of mayflies, stoneflies, caddis flies and midges can mean the difference in hooking fish and merely watching trout feed. This kind of knowledge will tell you when and where trout will feed, the size, shape and color of the flies to use and how to present them naturally to the fish. The same is true of warm water species like bass. Thorough knowledge of the bait fish, crustaceans and insects that inhabit the lakes, ponds and reservoirs will dramatically increase your effectiveness.

And, of course, this identification process is made more complex because fish are feeding on different things from top to the bottom within a single day and within the season due to many environmental factors. In early spring, for example, fish will seek the shallow water at mid-day because its warmth will attract a variety of food sources that are themselves attracted to the life there. In the heat of mid-summer, fish will forage those same shallows only in the cooler hours of early morning and late evening because of the water temperature. In the fall, the cycle will come full circle

and the needs of the fish will best be met in the same place again.

As you can see, determining what fish are feeding on at any given time can be very interesting in itself. Like so many other aspects of fly fishing, it can develop into a separate, self-sustaining interest. But, while it's true that it will take a considerable amount of time to master this subject, there are some shortcuts.

Fly Fishing for Trout, Fishing the Dry Fly and Tying Trout Flies

Take the mystery out of becoming a more successful trout angler no matter how long you've been fly fishing. Let Gary Borger, internationally known fly fishing author, be your personal instructor.

In Fly Fishing for Trout, *Gary demonstrates proven techniques for fishing dry flies, nymphs and streamers while fishing famous western rivers. In* Fishing the Dry Fly, *you'll see Gary's special dry fly techniques at work on the difficult fish of Armstrong's Spring Creek, the Madison River and the Henry's Fork of the Snake and learn how to book trout on your favorite stream. And, for those anglers who want to learn how to tie their own flies,* Tying Trout Flies *will teach you the fundamental techniques for dry flies, nymphs and streamers.*

Nymphing

Gary Borger's easy-to-use guide to identifying, tying and fishing artificial nymphs. The book presents a basic approach to all these techniques in one comprehensive lesson, covering both traditional and new theories about fishing the underwater fly. Casting, locating fish, detecting the strike, selecting tackle and making the proper presentation. A comprehensive view of this key angling technique.

Caddisflies

A major study by Gary LaFontaine of one of the most important aquatic insects to the fly fisher. The book introduces new patterns that impressionistically and effectively imitate the naturals, then gives detailed instructions on how best to fish larval, pupal and adult flies. Also, a comprehensive entomology of the important caddisfly species with emergence tables and distribution charts for representative trout streams in various parts of North America.

The Fish's Menu

Sometimes, you will be fortunate enough to find an experienced angler who will share information with you. Maybe that person will be a friend who will give you help or a professional guide who will share invaluable knowledge collected during thousands of hours on the water. Sometimes, if you're fishing a famous piece of water, you can often find books and magazines containing this information drawn from the writer's experiences.

But, if none of these sources is available, you can use a number of simple sampling techniques that are are really fun. Sometimes, if you're stream fishing, just turning over a few rocks will tell you a lot. Inexpensive nets can also be used to drag through the shallows where plants thrive and to find most of the foods the fish are pursuing. Whether it's insects, crustaceans, baitfish or whatever, be sure and record what you find.

Our Advice: Make careful note of the size, shape and color of the fish's food and how it moves which will help you select the right fly to match the food you find. But be sure to notice the numbers of what you find since the most abundant foods are the most likely items on the fish's menu and the first foods to imitate when you start fishing.

This approach is very helpful to anglers who fish freshwater streams—particularly those holding trout—because they are able to develop hatching charts for bugs trout feed on. Knowing, for example, that the Hendrickson mayflies will be hatching at 2 p.m. each day for the first two weeks in

Sampling Net and Kit

*I*f all this sampling stuff sounds like a lot of fun—particularly to you trout fanatics—you may now be asking yourself some very basic questions. "What about getting all the equipment you need to do it? Where do you get it? How much?"

Not to worry. For less than $5, you can be out there sampling with the pros.

Here's how:

The Net

Careful, now. This is where you may blow at least half your budget, so be creative. Head down to your favorite hardware store and find one of those guys who knows where everything is and what to do with it. Ask him for two dowels (one-inch diameter and three feet long), a sheet of window screen (three feet long and 18 inches wide) and a dozen small nails or tacks.

Then back to whatever functions as your workshop (a fly tying room will do just fine) and assemble. All you need is a small hammer. Simply spread the screen out on the floor and nail it to the end of each dowel so the narrow side of your screen runs half way up the dowels. To make this thing work, just stick the screen into the water until you reach bottom, then, standing upstream, loosen the gravel or sand with your feet. The critters in the water will drift into the screen and can be picked out when you lift up.

Preserving Bottles

What are you going to do with all those things you found in the stream? Why save them for later examination so you can identify them and, more importantly, tie or buy flies to match them.

And. to do that, you'll need a couple dozen little bottles. You can find the ideal bottle in any campus bookstore in the lab section. They're made of glass and have corks that plug the top. But any other small, clear bottles will do just fine. To preserve your specimens, fill the bottle with rubbing alcohol from your medicine chest or buy some at the drugstore.

It also makes sense to label your bottles so you can record where and when
(continued on page 18)

May is a great piece of information. The real advantage of this information is knowing on what and, approximately, when the fish will be feeding most actively before you get to the stream instead of figuring it out when you get there. This is particularly important for the trout fisher. This information also enables anglers to acquire the flies they'll need to imitate the foods they find before they travel to the stream.

Strategies for Selective Trout

Author Doug Swisher shows you how to make the evolutions from a capable angler to a master fly fisher. By combining your physical casting skills with the mental skills of knowing what strategies to use during hatch and no-hatch situations, you'll be able to catch selective trout when others can't. Let Doug show you: how trout select their food and how you can imitate it; his strategies for fishing a typical hatch from bottom to top and how to make super long drag-free presentations from any position.

Selective Trout

A truly revolutionary book on matching the hatch and taking selective trout on Eastern and Western rivers. Written by Doug Swisher and Carl Richards, this book gives descriptions on the no-hackle and paradun patterns, invaluable hatching charts covering the entire country and strategies for fishing the "super hatches."

Hatches

In the long tradition of books about insect hatches important to trout, Al Caucci and Bob Nastasi have put together the most comprehensive description of the mayfly hatches you'll encounter wherever you fish for trout. Lots of helpful information on mayfly behavior in all stages of maturity that will help you select the proper flies and make effective presentations. Solid, practical information plus fascinating scientific insights that will let you go as far as you want with this subject.

One important thing to keep in mind about hatching charts: though it sometimes looks like it, the natural world is not a mechanical world. Because of a variety of factors like temperature and water levels, hatches can come early or late during each season. But, with your charts, you'll be able to adjust your angling trips because all the hatches will follow the same sequence each year. They just don't always come at precisely the same times. A good source of such charts are fly fishing clubs and dealers who have already worked out the hatch cycles for local waters, saving you a lot of time. If you fish the blue ribbon waters a lot, there are a number of excellent books on the hatching cycles of these waters.

If you aren't interested in this type of activity and are content to take a more general approach, there is a broad rule to follow when identifying the best time of the day to go looking for fish. It's what Doug Swisher calls his "Pleasant Time of the Day" theory in his video. It states the hatch on any stream will probably occur during the time of the day when the weather is most pleasant to you. For example, during the early season when the weather is typically cold, the most pleasant time of the day is midday. In summer, it's early and late in the day. By fall, you're back to midday. This approach is especially helpful when fishing new waters and you have no knowledge of local hatches.

The key to successful sampling is to be disciplined enough to put down your rod and take out your sampling net.

Gathering this information can really be a fascinating part of fly fishing and many anglers even become expert entomologists. But don't worry. You don't have to be an expert. Just mastering the basics will help you be effective most of the time. Even if you don't pursue research and sampling to this degree, your efforts will make your days on the water far more productive. You'll know when fish are feeding, what

---

Sampling Net and Kit, cont.

you got your sample for later reference.

A Carrying Kit

You'll need something to carry your bottles and labels plus anything else that strikes your fancy like tweezers for grabbing tiny bugs and magnifying glasses. A small tackle box is perfect, but anything else you've got will do fine.

Remember you're not going for the Nobel Prize here. Just after a few bugs. Any variation on this approach will work fine and you can take this as far as you like. Anywhere from "A dark brown #12 nymph" to "*hexagenia limbata* nymph, light gray abdomen 17 millimeters long. . . " You get the idea: make it as fun as you like and use the information.

they're after and will have effective flies to take them all before you get on the water. That's quite a return on your investment of time.

Temperature and Oxygen

Another important factor in fish location is water temperature which influences the metabolism of all species. Fish are cold-blooded. This means that water temperature directly controls their body temperature and this in turn influences their activity level.

In early season, when the water is very cold, a fish's metabolic rate and demand for calories will be very low. Fish are poor feeders in these conditions. At times like these, only the most appealing of flies slowly retrieved or placed right on the nose of a fish will be taken on occasion. However, as the water warms and food becomes abundant, fish become more active feeders until higher temperatures limit their feeding activity to cooler periods of the day. By fall, when waters cool again, fish often go on a feeding binge just before their dormant period in winter.

Tied directly to this behavior pattern is the oxygen content in the water. The higher the water temperature, the less dissolved oxygen it can hold. So, as water begins to reach higher temperatures, its oxygen content goes down, driving fish to seek more oxygenated locations like riffles, pocket water and deeper, cooler pools. In moving water, these can be obvious places like deep pools, springs and shaded banks. But, in lakes, it can also be places like heavy concentrations of weeds and vigorous wave action which produce high levels of oxygen in the water. Warm temperatures will also cause fish to feed more actively in the earlier hours of the day when the water is cooler after a night of lower temperatures.

To give you a picture of how important temperature and oxygen are to fish behavior, let's look at the way they influence trout. At a range of 32 to 45 degrees, a trout's metabolism is so low that the fish are in a state of hibernation and are hardly breathing. As the water warms to 50 degrees, metabolism and feeding increase, while the 55 to 65 degree range is ideal for optimum feeding. But, as the water moves into the 68 to 75 degree level, a problem occurs: a trout's metabolism increases greatly, yet there is less oxygen in the water. By the time the temperature moves past 75 degrees, a trout will suffocate if it

WHAM
by Jim Kenyon

Clear, calm morning. Just a hint of a breeze.

Hairbug lands gently inches from the rock-edged shoreline. Pause. Twitch. Pause. . . WHAM! Three-pound smallmouth hangs from my thumb.

All this drifting through my mind working the St. Croix River in the cool of a July morning. But, so far, just a partial fantasy. Plenty of hairbugs up against the shoreline, plenty of Pause and Twitch. But no WHAM! Not a single WHAM!

It's all, Cast. Twitch. . . Twitch. . . Twitch. . . pause. Change fly, different pattern. Cast. Strip, Strip, Strip. Change fly, different color. Still no WHAM!

"Be patient," says the guide. "Sometimes it's slow starting. Sometimes they won't come up at all."

Patience, my ass. If I had the old spinning outfit, I go down after 'em.

But, wait a minute. I've got that spare spool with a Steelhead Wet Tip® III on it. The one my fishing partner said I'd use on the Bighorn in the fast runs. Never got to try it there. Too many fish. Don't have that problem here.

"What're ya trying now?" asks the guide, friendly but skeptical.

"One of those sinking tip lines for steelhead," I answered, threading line.

"No steelhead in the St. Croix," the guide says. (To himself? To me? No one?)

Olive Wooly Bugger blacktail tied on. Cast. Strip, Strip, Strip. Cast. . . pause. Strip. WHAM! Two-and-a-half pound smallie.

"Ha," says the guide. "Nice fish. I knew they were here!"

Cast, pause. . . Strip. WHAAAAM! Twin to the first smallmouth.

"How you fishing that?" asks the guide as he casts the hairbug, twitches it and pauses for the 753rd time without a WHAM!

I cast, pause, strip. WHAM! Third fish in eight casts.

"Damn," says the guide. "I don't suppose you have another one of those lines with you, do you?"

Though it sometimes looks like it, the natural world is not a mechanical world.

doesn't move to cooler, more oxygenated water.

Locating Fish—Saltwater Species

While the basic drives for protection and food extend to saltwater species, the big differences in salt and freshwater fish behavior is determined by the very different environments. Neither part of the familiar 90/10 rule (fish feed 90 percent of the time below the surface and are found in only 10 percent of the water) applies, since saltwater species rarely spend time feeding on or near the surface. In fact, some species never do come up.

To the angler accustomed to the intimacy of a trout stream or even large reservoirs filled with panfish, bass and pike, the vastness of the oceans is, at first glance, an angling scene too big to comprehend. Like so many things, however, a little knowledge makes this fly fishing universe much more manageable. Another big difference between fresh and saltwater fish is that everything happens faster—including your pulse! The speed of the fish, the need for quicker casts and, often, a faster retrieve. Finally, it is a much more complex food chain where Everybody is eating Everybody else!

What this all means is the saltwater flats angler pursues powerful, fast-moving fish in shallow water that test his ability to stalk them and make quick accurate casts. For most anglers, fishing to sighted fish combines the best of hunting and fishing skills and provides the ultimate angling challenge.

Another big difference between fresh and saltwater fish is that everything happens faster—including your pulse.

Fly Rodding for Tarpon and The Challenge of Giant Tarpon

Whether you've already had your first tarpon encounter or are still in the dreaming-about-it-stage, these two tapes are made for you. Featuring tarpon world-record holder, Billy Pate, who shares his knowledge learned from hooking over 4,000 tarpon, these tapes are your shortcut to becoming a knowledgeable tarpon angler fast. These tapes will help you avoid the "culture shock" many anglers experience when they hook up with their first tarpon and the problems they have tangling with one of these brutes.

Fly Rodding for Tarpon shows you how to spot tarpon, exactly what tackle you'll need and the casting techniques necessary to hook up with these silver kings of the salt. You'll learn where and when to cast and see which fly patterns and retrieves will consistently produce hook-ups. You'll then be guided through the skills you must have and the strategies you must know to land one of these super-charged fighting fish.

The Challenge of Giant Tarpon builds on the principles and techniques demonstrated in the first tape. Billy shows you how to make the transition from landing average-weight tarpon to fighting "box car" size silver kings. If you've ever dreamed what it's like to tangle with one of these huge fish weighing nearly 200 pounds, this is an exciting way to feel each strike and share in the thrill of every jump.

For the most part, saltwater fly fishers roam the shallow flats of the Atlantic and Pacific Oceans where they can stalk popular saltwater species like bonefish, tarpon, permit, snook and redfish. Typically, a flat is composed of one or more types of bottom like sand, mud, grass, live and dead coral and holds a great variety of small fish and crustaceans that make up the diet of these sport fish.

Inside and Outside Flats

There are two kinds of flats: "inside" and "outside." They are distinguished by the amount of wave action that determines the primary characteristics of each. An Outside Flat usually faces the ocean and receives constant wave action. This prevents sediment from accumulating, creating a hard bottom that is easy to wade. Inside Flats are usually protected from wave action by keys, islands and the mainland surrounding them. This allows sediment to build up on the coral floor, creating a mud or "ooze" bottom of various thicknesses and making wading difficult to impossible. Because of this condition these flats are fished primarily from skiffs.

There are features within each flat important to understanding fish behavior.

Valentine Atkinson

Almost to band. . . almost.

For example, many grassy flats—inside and outside—have a series of sandy, shallow holes usually a few inches deeper than the rest of the flat and an average of 20 feet in diameter. Known as "potholes," these areas, like prime lies of freshwater fish, are both resting places and feeding stations. A gamefish may sometimes lie inside a pothole facing the tide and wait for shrimp, crabs and small fish to drift in with the current, providing an easy meal. One of the most important areas of a flat is where it drops into deeper water as much as a few feet or as little as six inches. This is a likely spot to find fish cruising as they tail in the shallows with the protection of the deep water nearby.

No-Man's Land

Between the flats and the deep Blue Water is another world called No-Man's Land. Much different from the flats and deeper (from three to eight feet), it is usually located between the flat on the mainland side and a reef on the ocean side with a very hard bottom of coral, sponges, sea fans and turtle grasses. In this world, the sportfish find an abundance of crayfish

and stone crabs on the bottom and, in the cavities of sponges, thousands of snapping shrimp which periodically leave the safety of their lie and roam the flats to feed themselves. A good place for large species like tarpon and permit, No-Man's Land is also the place where schools of bonefish can hold during low tide, waiting for those extra few inches of water so they can come onto the flats to feed.

Within these areas holding the various gamefish fly fishers pursue, there are individual characteristics important to angling strategies.

For example, the type of bottom found in a flat indicates the type and coloration of food the fish will be feeding on, an important factor when selecting the correct fly to use. While a sand bottom does not support the quantity of life of a grass bottom, most sandy bottoms sustain an ample number of burrowing animals such as shrimp and crabs.

Tides

The one characteristic that constitutes the greatest difference between freshwater and salt fly fishers and, perhaps, the most important factor of all in saltwater angling is a clear understanding of tides. When water is moving strong across a flat, small baitfish and, especially, small crustaceans like the shrimp and crabs cannot swim against the tide. These small animals either drift freely or bury themselves in the flat's bottom or grasses. It is at this time when the fish move onto the flats from the deeper water, feeding against the tidal flow like a trout in a stream. Other times, the tide will bring an influx of cooler water to the flats and bring the temperature up to optimum feeding levels for fish or simply increase water clarity.

Nothing clears your head like a frosty steelhead morning.

Seeing with Expert Eyes

This brief overview of the environment of fresh and saltwater species indicates the complexity of the forces that influence fish behavior. A fascinating study in itself, the understanding of this world is essential to catching the fish you choose to pursue. And, as your knowledge of this world increases, so will your angling successes. Doors of perception will open wide and, when they do, the fish's world will continue to change for you as you see it through more expert eyes.

Presentation is what sets the master anglers apart from everyone else.

You will notice subtle puff of mud on the salt flat bottom you never saw before and it will tell you that the bone's are nearby. You will see the swallows move over the spring creek flats and know it's time to move into the water just before the first trout feeds on the surface. You will see a light circle the size of a dinner plate on the dark sand bottom of a cold, clear lake and know panfish bigger than the size of your hand will attack a fly sunk deep.

In time, you will learn to see what has always been there, what you always saw. But, now, it will have meaning for you, too. Like the hunters of old, you will read the signs of the quarry you seek, game you pursue for different reasons but with no less intensity or desire. And the signs will tell you what you need to know first. Where to find the fish.

Next, we'll continue to build your foundation of essential concepts by looking at the most critical part of the Formula for Success: Presentation.

Howard West

Presentation

"The more you practice—especially casting—the luckier you get."

We have arrived at the heart of fly fishing mastery. In this section, we'll examine the things that can have the most dramatic effect on your fishing and improve your angling success more quickly than any part of the Formula for Success.

With some guidelines on how to locate fish and determine the food they are most likely to eat, you're ready to explore the next part of our formula: Presentation. In the beginning stages of fly fishing, what this meant was getting into position near feeding fish or a likely looking spot and casting your fly in that direction. More advanced presentation techniques require a deeper understanding of the equipment—especially its range of effectiveness and limitations—and ways to use it. Ultimately, greater presentation skills mean greater casting expertise as well.

And the foundation of the high level casting skills you need to reach is a balanced fly fishing system. If you got started right, you have a system that consists of components designed to work together. This principle is absolutely essential to the development of your presentation skills and, if it's unfamiliar to you, please take a look at either the print or video version of SA's *Fly Fishing Made Easy* where we cover this in detail. The simple truth is that without such a system, you won't be able to present your fly correctly in different situations and conditions nor will you ever experience the pure joy that comes with casting a balanced system.

Of all the things we present, this part of the Formula is the most important. Its influence on your fishing experience cannot be emphasized too much. To put it another way: presentation is what sets the master anglers apart from everyone else. They don't have boxes full of secret fly patterns fish can't resist nor do they have x-ray vision that tells them where the fish are. What they do have is a clear understanding of the "Why" that will help them solve the angling riddles we all encounter in the field and they know how to choose and use the right equipment to solve those riddles in any situation or condition. Concentrating your efforts on presentation is the quickest way to improve your angling success.

Where We're Headed: Tackle and Techniques

What we're going to do first is discuss in detail the components of your fly fishing system. You need to understand what each piece of tackle can and—equally important—cannot do, so you can build a fly fishing system to meet your angling needs and success expectations now and as they grow in the future. Then you'll learn new techniques for using this equipment so you can make effective presentations in any angling situation under any conditions you might face.

In both aspects of presentation, the key to success is making the right choices from among the many available to you. It's not simply a matter of having lots of quality equipment or being able to make many different kinds of casts. The key to effective presentation is making the best choices of equipment and technique for the situations and conditions you face.

(By "situations," we mean the physical features like water depth, current speed or casting obstructions, while by "conditions," we mean nature's variables like wind or temperature.)

The Best Equipment

Not the most expensive equipment but what works best for the situation and condition

When you began to fly fish, you bought a line, a rod to match the line weight and a reel to hold the line. Next, came some leaders, tippets and flies. That got you started. Later, as you got more interested and tried some new techniques or fished for a new species, you added a fly line or

two. Maybe even a different weight rod and reel. And lots and lots of flies! That's taken care of your fishing needs for some time.

But, now, we want you to start looking at fly fishing tackle through expert eyes. To do that, you need to understand the way tackle design can influence your angling technique.

The Right Tackle for You

Because each piece of tackle does its job better than any other, it's very important that you learn the range of effectiveness and limitations of the tackle you own. As much as you may like your 5-weight system, for example, you've fished in enough situations to know you can't use it for everything. Think about those times you were forced to put on a bulky Muddler streamer because nothing else was working. Pushing it out 40 to 50 feet was murder, even without a breeze in your face.

You know the same is true of your floating line if you've ever tried to cast one with lots of heavy weight added to the leader. A small split shot or two works fine in some situations. However, if you need to add even more weight to get your fly to the fish, you're in big trouble. Casting becomes a graceless, chuck-and-duck process. When you push any piece of tackle beyond its range of effectiveness, you lose the control you need to present your fly properly.

At this stage of your angling development, you may have covered a lot of fishing situations with the tackle you own right now, but you probably didn't realize some problems in presentation were caused not by a lack of skill but by pushing your tackle beyond its range of effectiveness.

For example, you may have made your first trip out West armed only with your 5-weight system. And, when you fished those big elk hair caddis and humpies into a stiff breeze on the Yellowstone and found you couldn't put your fly where you wanted at your normal range—let alone reach those rises beyond—this was a problem not of casting skill but of using a line that didn't have enough carrying capacity to deliver your fly. Then, when they stopped hitting on top and your guide handed you a heavy, weighted wooly bugger, things really started to come apart!

So, while it's important to know what tasks each piece of equipment has been designed to perform, it is equally important to know the limitations of that equipment.

Let's start from the inside out.

Will Brewster

Don't hesitate to cut off old knots and re-tie them.

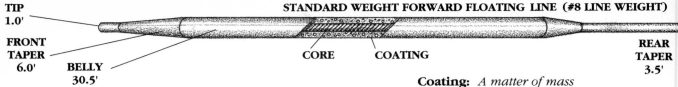

TIP
1.0'

FRONT
TAPER
6.0'

BELLY
30.5'

STANDARD WEIGHT FORWARD FLOATING LINE (#8 LINE WEIGHT)

CORE   COATING

REAR
TAPER
3.5'

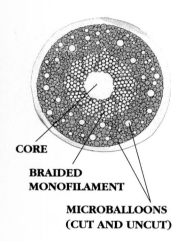

CORE

BRAIDED
MONOFILAMENT

MICROBALLOONS
(CUT AND UNCUT)

Anatomy of a Fly Line

Thanks to Scientific Anglers' introduction of modern fly lines, today's angler does not have to deal with the inconveniences and limitations of the old-fashioned silk lines that burdened past generations. After years of extensive laboratory research and field testing, we now have the most sophisticated and effective selection of lines available to any generation of fly fishers.

Unlike your fly rod, however, the design features of the modern fly line are difficult to recognize without optical assistance. So we'll give you compressed views of full length lines and a magnified cross sectional look that will enable you to see with expert eyes the differences in the anatomy of typical fly lines. We'll also tell you how these individual features can fill a particular angling need. All of this information will help you make the right decision when choosing lines for individual situations and conditions.

Basic Line Construction

Every line can be dissected into two parts: core and coating.

It is the modification of these parts that allows us to design lines with specific performance features to meet the needs of most any fly fishing situation or special condition. This is where science becomes critical to the art.

The Core: *Holding it all together*

The core of a fly line is primarily responsible for its tensile strength. Every fly line is built to be much stronger than the largest tippet normally used with that line. For example, a 2 or 3 weight line will test out at about 18 pounds, while the heaviest tippet used with such lines should be around 6 pound test. As you go higher up the line weight scale, the strength of the core increases proportionately. This means you'll always have a line strong enough to hold up under any fishing you might do with that line.

The construction and physical characteristics of the core material also have an impact on line performance. For example, by using a stiffer braided monofilament core material, we can make lines stiffer, like our Bonefish Taper, that won't become too limp in the intense heat so common on the flats.

Coating: *A matter of mass*

While the core is very important to the line's performance, the coating is where the wonders of science benefit the angler most. The coating is what gives a line its mass (weight). By modifying the coating and regulating how it is distributed along the length of the core, we can determine how a line performs: the power/delicacy of the line, how high it will float or quickly it will sink, its shootability, its durability and more. The coatings on SA lines are made from one of several pvc (polyvinylchloride) "platisol" bases we individually formulate in our Midland, Michigan plant.

Before we dive too deeply into the diversity of the coatings we manufacture, let's examine the anatomy of a typical fly line, taking a close look at the parts all lines have in common.

Every high performance fly line has a taper design. It's how the coating is shaped and distributed along the line. Let's take a look at the full profile of the basic taper designs. We'll start with the most popular WF floating line.

Nearly all WF lines have the individual sections shown in the illustration above. Here's what each one does:

• Tip: a short six to 12 inch level section where you attach your leader, this section's role is to protect the line's taper. Since many anglers cut off a small part of the fly line when they change leaders, the level tip allows these changes without shortening the front taper and altering the way the line casts.

• Front Taper: this is the section of the line that determines how delicately or powerfully the fly is delivered. Typically, four to eight feet long, it gradually decreases in diameter from the Belly section to the Tip. This graduation of the line's mass (weight) determines its ability to transfer your casting energy. (We'll talk more about the importance of the front taper and the rest of the following fly line parts in the Design section.)

• Belly: this large diameter section is where most of the weight of a line is located and, consequently, where your casting energy is carried.

• Rear Taper: gradually decreasing in diameter from the thicker belly section to the much smaller diameter running line

**RUNNING
LINE
42.5'**

section, the rear taper creates the transition so important for casting smoothness and control.

• Running Line: this section exists primarily to make distance casting easier. Double Taper lines, which do not have a running line, connect identical front tapers at each end of the line. This large diameter belly line does not shoot well because it is heavy and increases surface contact with the rod guides. The running lines on Weight Forward lines, however, are small in diameter, creating little resistance and friction when shooting line. They are also lightweight, an important factor in shootability because the momentum and mass of the portion of the line moving through the air must pull the running line out through the guides.

• Head: this part is really the combination of front taper, belly and rear taper. Shooting Tapers are basically short lines consisting only of the first 30-foot section of a WF line and must be attached to a separate shooting line in order to be used. Such lines, when combined with an Ultra[2] shooting line or monofilament, are capable of making the longest distance casts, though accuracy and control are not as great as with conventional lines.

Design
The key to building lines with specific performance advantages

The performance advantages of one line over another are primarily the result of modifications in one or more of these areas: taper design, coating formulation or the characteristics of the core material. Balance is the key.

The easiest of the three to work with is the core material. Design is fairly straight forward. How stiff (like a Bonefish Taper) or supple (like our Air Cel®) a line needs to be and how much stretch a line must have to fish properly is mainly a function of the characteristics of the core material itself.

The next least complicated is **taper** design. Designing tapers for specific performance characteristics is primarily a matter of the relationships between line diameter and the length of the individual taper sections. To help you understand how we use taper design to give you lines with different fishing performance advantages, let's examine how each of the above taper sections can be modified. We'll use the standard Ultra[2] above as a comparson.

Let's start with a closer look at the front taper. Two lines of the same weight, but designed for different advantages will have different front taper lengths. For example, a standard WF-8-F Ultra line has a six foot taper, while a WF-8-F Bass/SWT Ultra line has a four foot taper. Generally speaking, the shorter front taper of the Bass/SWT design allows more momentum to be transferred from its belly section section to its tip and, thus, has more energy to turn over bass-size flies.

Bass Bug Taper
BBT/SWT

Lines with longer bellies are best for situations that require longer, accurate casts with great control. Such lines, however, can be a disadvantage at medium distances since they won't shoot as well as a standard WF line because the large diameter belly line with its greater surface area creates more friction in the guides. Lines with shorter bellies, like our Bass/SWT, Bonefish, Tarpon Tapers and Monocores, are designed to make the quick casts so necessary in saltwater angling. In these situations, the belly section is out of the guides after one or two false casts and shoots much better than the standard long belly WF lines. They do not, however, give you the long distance control or accuracy of the standard lines.

Shooting Taper   ST

A short rear taper of three feet, like we use on our Bonefish Tapers, helps when you need to cast quickly because the running line is in the guides sooner. A longer rear taper is best when you need both distance and line control because you get a smoother transmission of momentum from running line to belly. And, once the line is on the water, you can more easily mend and roll cast because there is more mass in the line at the tip of the rod. The new floating SA Steelhead Tapers are excellent examples of what a long rear taper can do. With their extra long 25-foot rear tapers, these lines produce exceptional long distance casting and mending performance.

Double Taper   DT

The critical design factors of the running line are its diameter, which is a function of the core's diameter and the thickness of the coating, and the stiffness

What is critical to performance in the vertical plane is being able to make lines with a variety of precise sink rates.

characteristics of the core itself. Everything else being equal, the smaller the diameter of the running line, the farther the line will shoot. Yet, the balance between the coating thickness and its durability must be considered because the running line has less coating relative to the rest of the line and, yet, is subject to the same or more abuse. This is why wear and tear often shows up here first.

Where science comes most heavily into play is in the coating formulation.

The complexity of formulating just the right line coating to meet your needs is where our R&D people have all the fun. It's a real balancing act and our guys are great jugglers. A sane man would soon become a little crazy after a few hours of listening to the "plastic string" boys arguing

A high-visibility line is easy to follow in the air and on the water.

over the merits and relationships of plasticisors to plastisol, the specific gravity comparisons of lead and tungsten, the balance of coating stiffness and the need for elasticity—just for starters. Sometimes, it seems a wonder that any prototype lines actually get produced, let alone agreement reached on actual new models for the market. Ah, the joys of science!

What all the juggling boils down to is pretty much formulating a coating that will deliver the desired performance, be durable enough to provide lasting value and, of course, be consistently reproducible from a manufacturing standpoint. Now, let's take a look at how fly line performance in both

the vertical (depth) and the horizontal (distance) planes is affected by the balance of ingredients that comprise the line coating.

Performance in the vertical plane is primarily a function of density.

How high a line floats or how fast it sinks is controlled by adding different densities of materials to the coating formulation.

Basically the relationship is this: the more microballoons the coating contains, the lower the line's density becomes, allowing it to float higher. Some of our lines also contain additional ingredients to further increase the floating properties. The Ultra[2]'s formulation (patent pending), for example, utilizes a unique chemistry that allows the line's surface to actually repel water. Consequently it floats higher and is easier to pick up off the water than any other line.

Conversely, to make a sinking line, we add higher density material to the coating formulation to make the line heavier than water. Many years ago, we pioneered the very expensive use of tungsten because it is denser than lead but much less toxic and harmful to the environment. This is one of the reasons we can make the fastest sinking lines on the market. What is critical to performance in the vertical plane is being able to make lines with a variety of precise sink rates. The key is the ability to add exact amounts of tungsten to the formulation. This enables us to offer sink rates from one inch per second (ips) to 10 ips so you can cover situations from fishing a nymph just below the surface to dredging the depths.

What fly line chemistry can do to increase fly line performance in the horizontal plane, shootability, primarily centers around reducing the line's COF (coefficient of friction). Simply stated: we reduce the friction of the line in the guides by adding special lubricants to the line's formulation. Ultra[2]'s coating has these special lubricants and, as a result, does not require frequent applications of line dressing, as some lines, to keep it performing well. It actually lubricates itself.

When you think about how much abuse a fly line gets in a normal day's fishing, it's a wonder that they last as long as they do. Consider a day in the life of a fly line belonging to a trout fisher: it's pulled out of a car trunk where temperature can exceed 150 degrees and cast into a stream at 65 degrees. It's dragged through the dirt over rocks and brush, hung up in wide assortment of foliage and stretched nearly to its breaking point while jerking the fly free after an errant cast, all the time being subjected to the harsh ultraviolet exposure of the sun, intermittently, albeit accidentally, being bathed in DEET, the number one culprit in premature death of a fly line, and all too infrequently stretched along its entire length as a trophy fish takes the angler to his backing. If all this weren't enough abuse heaped on the fly line, consider the curling effect of countless tight loops or, with a hurried cast, the supersonic stress of cracking the line like a whip.

So, you see, there is more to designing a quality fly line than simply making it cast well, float high and sink fast. It must also be durable and tough enough to be the best in laboratory tests and on your water. And that takes science. Lots of it.

Lines

When looking at the way lines are designed, there is one principle that's very important to understand when you're choosing a line for a specific situation or condition. A line is designed with an effective range and, as you reach the limits of that line's effectiveness, you should switch to another line density. If, for example, you are fishing the shallows of a lake (two to four feet deep), a floating line with a little split shot or a weighted fly will get your fly near the bottom just fine.

But, if you need to fish in deeper water (over four feet), you are moving beyond the effective range of your floating line for

Line Durability

*I*n 1986 we introduced our Monocore, a unique line with a clear, single strand monofilament core and coating. Whether you're fishing freshwater or salt, whatever the species, it's simply the most effective sinking line there is for casting to spooky fish in clear water. Interestingly, though, we didn't come up with the idea. The Shakespeare Company did. They introduced these lines many years ago, but soon stopped making them because their coating kept separating from the monofilament core.

But, serious saltwater anglers kept pleading for us to make this line and one of the "string boys," Bruce Richards, thought we could build one that would hold up better. We tried. The lines looked great, cast like bullets, but they just couldn't stand up to normal angler abuse. It didn't take long before the coating broke loose from the core. For awhile, we had lots of long faces around the bunsen burner!

Then, we started the networking process within 3M's technical community to find the person who had the answer to our monocore coating problem. When we bring the 3M braintrust into the discussions, we can call on some mighty heavy intellectual firepower.

In 3M's worldwide headquarters in St. Paul, we have more Ph.D.'s in one location than many major universities—over 2,500. They specialize in everything from Laser Imaging to Computer Sciences to Mass Spectroscopy. Obviously, they don't all work on fly lines. In fact, of the more than 70,000 different products 3M makes, Scientific Anglers accounts for only a few hundred. Yet, all the technical knowledge and scientific discoveries in the total R&D community are available to us. (Last year, 3M's R&D tab came to nearly one billion dollars!) That's why our lab guys always feel, no matter how complex the question, someone at 3M has the answer. The challenge is with over 5,000 R&D people in St. Paul alone, where do we start?

The most difficult part was explaining to contact after contact what a fly line was and why—of all things—3M was in the fishing business! In a few months, we were hot on the trail of our man and, before the season was over, we had him. Although an authority on adhesion promoters from our Adhesions, Coatings and Sealers Lab, Chuck Wright had never cast a fly, but he had the answer to many a fly fisher's dream. Following Wright's advice, we were able to boost the adhesion of our monocore coating by nearly 300%, making them almost as tough as our floating line.

This is just one little episode in the many ways 3M's science can help your art.

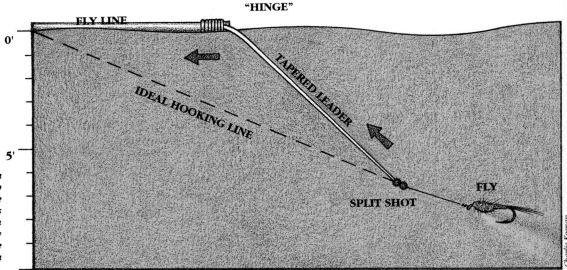

"HINGE"

FLY LINE

0'

IDEAL HOOKING LINE

TAPERED LEADER

5'

SPLIT SHOT

FLY

Charlie Keenan

A common problem when fishing a floating line with a weighted leader: the "hinge effect" prevents direct contact between you and your fly. The new Uniform Sink lines have eliminated this problem entirely.

three main reasons. First, you will not have good casting control because the weight is concentrated in one spot and even great line speed will not overcome this problem. Second, because the floating line stays on top, the fly is pulled away from the bottom toward the surface as you retrieve and, consequently, it's difficult to keep your fly deep. And, third, with a floating line, the deeper the fly, the more difficult it is to feel a strike because the "hinge" between the fly and the line creates so much slack. Depending on depth, a sinking tip or full sinking line with the appropriate sink rate will do the job far better.

Our Advice: The deeper you need to go to reach the fish, the more imperative it is to use a sinking line.

What happens if the fish go out of the shallows into deeper water? You'll need to start exploring the water with a full sinking line like a Wet Cel® II, retrieving it at progressively greater depths until you start getting hits. If the fish are in four to 10 feet of water, the Wet Cel® II will get your fly to them in a reasonable amount of time. But, if the fish have moved into deeper water yet, you'll need an even faster sinking line to avoid excessive waiting for your fly to reach the fish.

To fish effectively, you need to be able to present your fly in a full range of situations and conditions. You can only do this with additional fly lines. And, equally important to owning the right lines for the fishing you do, is knowing the range of effectiveness and limitations of each of those lines.

Line Weight: *A matter of mass*
When selecting the line weight of your

system, your first step is to match the system with your specific angling needs. (For those who haven't yet put their cash on the counter, please look at a copy of our *Fly Fishing Made Easy* to eliminate a lot of frustration) If most of your fishing will be with large, bushy flies, for example, you'll need a line at the heavier, power end of the line weight spectrum because the greater wind resistance such flies create must be overcome by the weight of the line. A small fly, however, has little wind resistance and will be better presented with a lighter line for a more delicate presentation. Or, if distance is an important factor,

A magical moment on the Henry's Fork.

Valentine Atkinson

Bluegill University

by Bruce Richards

I love fly fishing. If I could only do one kind of fishing the rest of my life, I'm sure it would be trout. But, if I had to make that choice, I know the fish I'd miss most would be bluegills!

Most anglers think of bluegills as pretty and dumb. They think all you have to do is tie on an old, worn-out trout fly and put your fly on the water to fill up your bucket with 'gills. On some days, that can happen. Especially with small fish. But big bluegills are another matter. To take those big ones (hand-size and larger), you'll have to go below the surface and use your best presentation skills to be successful.

There's a small lake in northern Michigan not far from where we manufacture the Scientific Anglers lines. It's a walk-in lake, so it doesn't get much pressure. That's probably one reason why it holds good populations of bass and bluegills. The other is the abundant growth of lily pads and submerged weedbeds that provide perfect habitat for the fish in fairly shallow water. The bluegills are here and the big ones are always tough—even on calm days when the little ones are feeding on top—because they continue to feed below the surface.

On a very special day in May, 1987, I learned a lot about presentation from the big bluegills in this "secret" lake.

I hiked in with my canoe that day which was cool and windy—pretty typical for that time of year. Even though I was there to field test products, I started with my usual routine. I wanted to fish the lily pads and weed beds that grew in four to six feet of water near shore and I planned to use the small nymphs the bluegills seemed to favor. Using my 12-foot 5X leader on an Ultra[2] floating line, I fished the shoreline for over an hour with limited success. Only a couple of small ones that somehow hooked themselves.

Something was not right. I seemed to be out of touch with the fishing. Literally. So I stopped and thought about the situation. My floating line was on the surface, while the weighted fly sank, pulling the leader down behind it. I guessed I was missing strikes because I didn't have a direct connection to the fly. The line was on the surface, but the leader and fly were angled down making a 45-degree angle where the leader and line connect. This "hinge" in the system created a big problem. It prevented direct contact between me and the fly, greatly decreasing my feel for strikes. With spring bluegills that need a slow retrieve and hit light, I would not take fish as long as I had the hinge in my line.

In addition to this problem, I had the wind. It wasn't blowing hard, but hard enough to put a chop on the surface that made it impossible to see a strike whether I watched the line tip or used a strike indicator. All I saw was a constantly bobbing, bouncing line that would tell me nothing when a fish struck. To further complicate matters, the gusting wind would blow my line across the surface, putting a belly in it. This reduced my contact with the fly even more and made a slow, controlled retrieve impossible. It was frustrating to know fish were there—probably feeding on my fly from time to time—and I couldn't tell when they struck.

If a floating line wasn't the answer, maybe a full sinking line would solve the problem. A Wet Cel® I—a slow sinking line—eliminated the effect of wind on my floating line and improved my success somewhat. But I still had that sagging belly in the line. Like other conventional sinking lines, the Wet Cel's belly section sinks faster than the tip section, causing the line to sink in a "U" shape with the tip section riding high. This sag kept me from feeling most of the soft strikes of those big bluegills. The only time I could hook fish was when I happened to retrieve line the same time the fish ran with the fly. With these odds stacked against me, I would be a loser all day long!

Suddenly, the odds shifted dramatically *(continued on page 30)*

(continued on page 30)

choose a heavier weight line because it's easier to cast farther than a light one.

Below is a basic chart that will guide your decisions.

Line Function: *A matter of density*

Based on dedicated research and development on waters around the world, Scientific Anglers has produced lines that would have been inconceivable to previous generations. Today, you have lines that allow you to fish not only at greater depths but also fish for a broader range of species than ever before.

Presentation Delicacy → *Presentation Power*

3 & 4 weight lines, in double tapers and weight forwards, offer the ultimate in presentation delicacy. Their low weight and small silhouette make them ideal for casting small flies to spooky trout. However, they may be difficult to cast in windy conditions.
Generally, these lines are designed for fishing flies in sizes 14 to 28 with tippets of 4X to 8X.

5 weight lines are a bit of a compromise for the trout fisherman because some delicacy is lost. However, the added weight makes it easier to cast a wider range of fly sizes, including small to medium-size streamers. A 5 weight line is ideal for trout and panfish anglers who don't require extremely long casts.
5 weight lines are usually used with dry flies in sizes 12 to 22 and streamers in size 4 and smaller with tippets of 3X to 7X.

6 & 7 weight lines represent the midpoint of the delicacy/power presentation scale. They're ideal for casting larger, more wind-resistant trout flies, even under windy conditions like those found on many western streams. Because of their weight, they're the choice of the trout fishermen who fish primarily with streamers. For the bass fishermen who require more delicacy than power, 6 and 7 weight lines are also available in a bass bug taper. 6 and 7 weight lines are ideally used with dry flies and nymphs in sizes 8 to the very smallest and bass flies ands streamers in sizes 2 and smaller with a tippet of 0X to 5X.

8 & 9 weight lines definitely swing to the power side of the scale. They are most often used by the trout or salmon fishermen who need the added power to cast large, heavy flies. These lines, in bass bug tapers, are the preferred choice of bass fishermen who cast large, wind-resistant bugs. For light tackle saltwater enthusiasts, 8 and 9 weight lines are also available in saltwater tapers. These lines are usually used for fishing bass bugs and saltwater flies as well as large dry flies and streamers in sizes 3/0-4 with a tippet of 2X or larger.

10-15 weight lines are all at the brute power end of the presentation scale where delicacy is nearly out of the question. Their primary purpose is to cast very large, wind-resistant flies and poppers with maximum effectiveness. These lines are the number one choice of anglers who do a lot of saltwater fishing where long casts are often a necessity. Weight forward saltwater tapers are available for the line weights 10-12.
10-12 weight lines are most often used for fishing salmon and saltwater flies in sizes 4/0-2 with a tippet of 0X or larger.

Bluegill University, cont.

in my favor. I remembered I had brought along some experimental lines that we had just made up at the SA plant earlier in the week. These lines had graduated densities that allowed the tip section to sink slightly faster than the belly section. In theory, this would eliminate the sag in the belly and allow the line to sink with the tip down. This "straight" line shape would give me a more direct contact with the nymph I was fishing and would enable me to feel those light-striking bluegills.

Using these new prototype lines—they are SA's new Uniform Sink lines—and a shorter six-foot leader, I was able to fish a very slow retrieve and maintain a direct feel of my fly. With this set up, I could swim my nymph across the tops of submerged weed beds and tease out those big bluegills. Once I found the depth where these fish were feeding, I cast over the beds, let my line sink to the feeding level, then began my retrieve. I am happy to report I hooked and released over a dozen big bluegills (nine to11 inches). I felt more light strikes and was able to hook fish consistently. And need I add: it was fun.

Since that day in the classroom on the little lake in northern Michigan, I've fished the Uniform Sink lines for all kinds of fish. Bass, trout, steelhead and salmon. Even saltwater species. There's no doubt in my mind about the lessons I learned that day. I'm able to take more fish with this line because I miss very few fish, no matter how light the strike. It's no longer academic. You can get all the proof you need. Just try a Uniform Sink line on your favorite species.

Floating Lines (F)

The floating line is the basic tool for fly fishing because you can productively fish a fly on or near the surface for a wide variety of species. Whether it's trout, bass, panfish, Atlantic Salmon, shad or many varieties of saltwater fish, they all feed on or near the surface at times. In addition to its versatility, the floating line is also the easiest line to fish and most enjoyable. Easy to cast and pick up off the water to re-cast, you can follow the drift of your floating line and watch the exciting takes of your fly on top.

When choosing a floating line, there are three important features you'll want to consider: floatability, shootability and durability. Although difficult to see, there are differences in the way floating lines ride on the surface. Higher is better because it's less likely to be pulled under by the current and makes it easier to pick off the water for the next cast without spooking fish. The best lines have a coating that allows the line to slide easily through the rod guides for greater line control and casting distance. And, finally, you'll want a line that will hold up in the field and give many seasons of high performance before it begins to wear out.

Although the standard floating tapers are unsurpassed for handling a broad range of typical situations and conditions, they do have limitations. Long ago, we addressed this problem and, through the years, have designed new generations of specialty lines that give high performance in specialized situations and give you the extra edge you'll need for success. For more information see the section on Specialty Lines in this chapter.

Sinking Lines (S)

Unless your fishing interests are very narrowly focused on shallow streams or surface feeding fish only, the exclusive use of floating lines severely limits your approach to fly fishing success. If not, a whole new world awaits you! Because an angler who uses a floating line exclusively spends 90 percent of their time casting a line over the heads of feeding fish, particularly the big ones. Your only choice when they're not on top is to cast and hope the fish decide to come up. Otherwise, your fishing time is just spent practicing your casting. So, to spend your valuable time productively, you'll need to learn how to use some type of sinking line. Specifically, the goal is to put your fly at the feeding

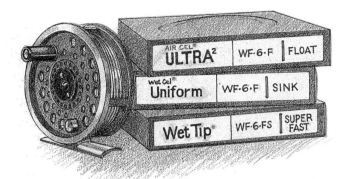

level of the fish and keep it there as long as possible.

To help you do this, we offer two different designs of full length sinking lines. The standard Wet Cel® that has been the traditional favorite and the new Wet Cel® Uniform Sink series. Both are available in a wide range of sink rates and will get your fly to the fish. The Uniform Sink lines just do it differently. In fact, so differently that many anglers say they are the most revolutionary development in sinking lines over the last 20 years.

All traditional weight forward sinking lines have more of their dense coating material in the belly section than the tip because of taper design. Consequently, the thicker belly section is denser and sinks faster than the thinly coated small diameter tip section. The result is belly sag between you and the fly. To feel a strike with these older design sinking lines, you first have to retrieve in the belly sag or the fish must hit hard enough to pull it out. In contrast with the new Uniform Sink lines, the tip is actually a slightly higher density than the belly and sinks faster, straighter so you are in more direct contact with your fly. In short, we all have been missing a lot of strikes over the years.

Years ago, some of the top stillwater trout anglers in the world like Hal Janssen, Randall Kaufmann and Hughie McDowell as well as deep water bass fan, Jimmy Nix, asked us for a line that would sink straighter. Our lab went to work and the plant cranked out generation after generation of prototype lines for testing until our field testers got what they wanted.

The first-time Uniform Sink user notices two big differences right away. First, because the belly sag is eliminated, they feel in more direct contact with their fly. In fact, their most frequent comment is, "I'm surprised how much more sensitive these

The three basic types of line—floating, sinking and sinking tip—should be part of every fly line system.

The exclusive use of floating lines severely limits your approach to fly fishing success.

lines are. I feel strikes that I would have missed before." The benefit is, of course, more solid hook-ups. The second thing they notice is the Uniform Sink lines cost about the price of a dozen flies more than the "saggers." Yet, it's no surprise that no one has asked for their money back! After all, the line will last through years of hard use and help you land more fish. The flies, on the other hand, may not last the season if they are "hot." If not, how smart was the investment, especially if you don't have the right line to get them in front of the fish.

So, where does this leave you if you are already equipped with a full selection of standard Wet Cel® lines?

Our Advice: Switch over as soon as practical for your most frequently used densities, especially Wet Cel III® (Hi-D®) or faster sink rates because line sag is most pronounced in the higher density lines. Then, as your old standard Wet Cel® lines wear out or get passed along to friends or family, replace them with new Uniform Sink models.

With traditional sinking lines, the belly section sinks faster than the tip, creating sag (shaded section) that causes you to miss a lot of strikes. With Uniform Sink lines, the tip is slightly heavier than the belly, letting your line sink without sag and giving you direct contact with your fly.

Like the various choices in line weight, sinking lines come in different sink rates (SA offers six) designed to get your fly to fish in any situation or condition you may face. To select the right line, you'll also need to understand the effective range and limitations of each line's sink rate so you can get your fly to fish and keep it there. Because water depth, current speed and rate of retrieve all influence the sink rate, we have designed lines with different sink rates so you can choose the one with a range of effectiveness that meets your individual angling need. As you move beyond the limits of one line, there will be another line that will sink faster and get your fly where you want it.

The first step in this process is to start thinking about fish location vertically as well as horizontally. By this we mean you must consider not only how *far* to cast but also how *deep* the line must go and how *fast* it must get there.

In some instances, you will be able to use a floating line to fish below the surface very successfully. For example, when fishing for trout or smallmouth in a moderately swift stream with a maximum depth of three to four feet, adding split shot to your leader will usually get your fly to the fish effectively. But, if you begin to fish water with greater depth or current speed, you will need to use some type of sinking line to get the job done. In simplest terms, the need varies by situation and technique.

If you are fishing a nymph upstream, for example, a floating line with weight is the best choice because using this tech-

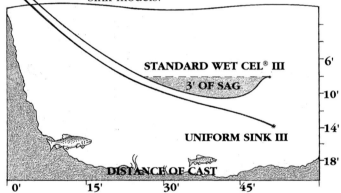

SIX SINK RATE OPTIONS

SLOWEST

FASTEST

Sink Rates:	Lines:				Line Weights:					
		5	6	7	8	9	10	11	12	13
1.25-1.75 ips	Wet Cel® Intermediate	•	•	•	•	•	•	•	•	•
1.50-2.50 ips	Wet Cel® Uniform Sink I	•	•	•	•	•	•			
	Wet Cel® I	•	•	•	•	•	•			
1.75-3.00 ips	Wet Cel® Uniform Sink II	•	•	•	•	•				
	Wet Cel® II (WF)	•	•	•	•	•	•	•	•	•
2.50-4.25 ips	Wet Cel® Uniform Sink III		•	•	•	•	•			
	Wet Cel® III (Hi-D®)			•	•	•	•	•		
3.75-6.25 ips	Wet Cel® Uniform Sink IV		•	•	•	•	•			
	Wet Cel® IV (Hi-Speed Hi-D®)	•	•	•	•	•	•	•		
4.50-6.00 ips	Wet Cel® V Uniform Sink			•	•	•	•			

nique lets the fly fall freely and get deep quickly. Yet, for other nymphing techniques, you'll need some type of sinking line to get your fly to the fish. The Brooks method—up and across, then fish the swing—and the traditional wet fly steelhead method—quartering downstream—are most effective with some type of sinking tip line. Since the fly follows the line, the floating portion of the line acts as an indicator of strikes. It also makes mending easy.

Advanced Strategies for Selective Trout

This tape will show you how to reach the highest plateau of angling mastery. Doug Swisher refines the techniques of "Strategies for Selective Trout," shows you how to master specialized techniques for no-hatch situations like streamer fishing and cover more water in less time. You'll also learn how to stack mend for the ultimate deep nymphing fishing, learn to tell what trout are feeding on during multiple hatch periods and fine-tune your presentation skills to catch trout when they're midging.

In situations like stillwater fishing where a full sinking line is the best choice, anglers will typically use the "countdown" method to systematically locate fish. Simply cast your fly to where fish are most likely holding and, when your fly hits the water, start counting slowly to a specific number such as five, then begin your retrieve. After fishing at the Five Count level for awhile and not getting any strikes, let your fly sink deeper to the 10 Count level. Then, if you start getting hits, simply recast and let the line sink down for a 10 Count. Now, you're in business.

Once the feeding depth is located, then you can use a faster or slower sink rate line to keep your fly at the desired level longer. For example, if you're using a 7-weight

Uniform Sink III (sink rate: 2.75 ips) and you start hitting the fish five counts below the surface, the line's sink rate is so fast, your fly will quickly sink past the fish. A better choice, then, would be a slower sinking line like the Uniform Sink I (sink rate: 1.75 ips) to keep the fly at the right feeding level longer. Remember, there are two ways to get a faster sink rate: use another faster sinking type line (a Wet Cel IV® is faster than a III) or choose a heavier weight line of the same type (an 8-weight Wet Cel IV® with a sink rate of 4.40 ips is faster than a 6-weight Wet Cel IV® with a sink rate of 3.75 ips).

Different Sink Rates

In the past, most anglers started out with a Wet Cel II®. Now, we advise buying a Uniform Sink II (1.75-2.75 ips). This line will handle most fishing needs below the surface of stillwaters down to about eight to 10 feet. It gives the angler the ability to fish different levels and not spend unreasonable amounts of time waiting for the fly to reach fish and also hooks fish more effectively. But experience will quickly teach you that you need to have additional lines with faster sink rates to extend their effective range.

While it is true that in most stillwater instances one sinking line such as the Uniform Sink II will eventually get your fly to the fish, you will find many situations where its relatively slow sink rate greatly limits your chances. For example, you will find that fish often move quickly when feeding beneath the surface and, to present your fly effectively, you'll need to get it to their feeding level in a hurry. Otherwise, the fish may have left the feeding area by the time your fly reaches them.

Lines with faster sink rates will sometimes help you take more fish during those frenzied but short-lived feeding periods. When you've located feeding fish at deeper levels, you will not want to sit there waiting 45 seconds for your fly to get back down to those fish! And, finally, you will discover that in deeper water with fast-moving currents, your fly may never get to the fish no matter how far upstream you cast or how often you mend if you do not have a line with a fast enough sink rate.

For the angler committed to fishing still water, a complete system of sinking lines is essential for angling success because of the precise control they offer in presenting your fly to the fish at very specific feeding levels.

A weary steelhead comes to net after a long, hard fight.

Howard West

If you're having difficulty locating any of our products, call us. We'll put you in touch with the nearest Scientific Anglers dealer.
1-800-525-6290

With the proper choice of sink rate, you can get your fly down quickly to feeding fish and keep it there for the length of a long retrieve. The long retrieve, like a long, drag-free float of a dry fly, will increase the time you expose your fly to feeding fish and improve your catch rate. It's just a more efficient way to fish.

The objective in all line selection is to choose the line with a sink rate that will get your fly down to the level of feeding fish at the fastest speed and keep it there the longest.

Sinking Tip Lines (F/S):
The best of both worlds

Eventually, after you've experimented and fished with floating and sinking lines, you'll find yourself in situations where neither one is really the right choice.

In most stream fishing, for example, where line control on the water is very important, a full sinking line can cause problems. Since the full length of the line sinks, it cannot be mended to improve the drift of the fly and, on streams with complex currents, this can make it almost impossible to properly present your fly.

The main drawback to using a full sinking line, however, is the time and effort it takes to retrieve the sunken line for the next cast. The deeper the line goes down, the more line you have to bring up. Roll casting will bring your sinking line to the surface, but unfortunately, there's a lot of movement that may spook fish feeding nearby. Your only alternative is to strip in line until you're able to lift it out of the water.

On the other hand, with a floating line, your casting accuracy is improved and top water mending is easy. But it still has obvious limitations for subsurface fishing. It's virtually impossible to put enough weight on the fly and leader to sink it to the deeper feeding levels without causing serious casting problems.

Because of these limitations of both sinking and floating lines, Scientific Anglers developed a full selection of dual density (combination floating/sinking) lines called sinking tip lines. The higher density front section sinks the fly, while the floating rear section allows you to mend the line and watch the motion of the line on the surface for indications of a strike.

Although the depth these lines will sink is somewhat limited by the planing effect of the faster moving surface water, the control

advantages they offer make them the best choice in many stream situations. The F/S Wet Tip® lines, for instance, are particularly effective when fishing hot spots where your retrieve is relatively short. And, because only the front section sinks, sinking tip lines are easier to pick up for the next cast, helping you cover a lot more water.

In deciding which line is best for you in a specific situation, you will need to consider current speed, depth of water and rate of retrieve—just like full sinking lines. When nymph fishing in a fairly shallow stream with slow to moderate current, for example, a Wet Tip II® line would be the best choice, while a Wet Tip III® (Hi-D®) line would be better when fishing a stream with faster or deeper current. In the fastest currents or when you need to go deepest fastest, the Wet Tip® IV (Hi-Speed® Hi-D®) is the line of choice.

For information on using sinking tip lines, see Mastery Series tapes: "Strategies for Selective Trout," "Advanced Strategies for Selective Trout" and Steelhead Titles.

A System of Lines

Once they understand the advantages of subsurface fishing, most anglers are eager to explore the challenges and rewards of fishing with multi-line systems. But they are immediately faced with an apparent dilemma: of the hundreds of fly lines available (SA makes over 400 different lines), how do they build a system that's right for their angling needs?

The first step in finding your way is to sort your options by line density/sink rate.

This simple chart helps you reduce the options from 400 to 11 line options for an 8-weight system. These lines can then be broken into sub categories of floating, sinking tip and full sinking lines. Following the principle that each line does something better than any other line, you'll need to select those lines for your system that match the fishing you do. This solution would be fine if we always fished the same situations and conditions. But, for most anglers, one of the great joys of the sport is the new challenges it offers. Learning to take their favorite species in a dynamic environment and, especially, fishing in new locations create the need for a variety of lines.

There are two basic approaches to this process.

Some anglers buy lines based on what they know about the fishing they plan to do, hoping they will be effective for all the

The goal is to have the lines that will enable you to present your fly from top to bottom and anywhere in between.

Twelve 8-Weight Line Options

Floating Line:
- One of the Air Cel® Family

Sinking Lines:
- Wet Cel® Intermediate
- Wet Cel® I
- Wet Cel® II
- Wet Cel® III
- Wet Cel® IV
- Wet Cel® V (Uniform Sink only)

Sinking Tip Lines:
- Wet Tip® Intermediate
- Wet Tip® II
- Wet Tip® III
- Wet Tip® IV
- Wet Tip® V (Steelhead Taper only)

situations and conditions they encounter. As part of their planning for a trip to Alaska, for example, they buy one sinking tip line to fish for salmon as they travel up the river that guides them from the ocean to their spawning redds as well as the rainbows that hold tight to the bottom downstream, waiting for drifting eggs. This one-line approach may be fine for this very specific type of fishing. But anglers may discover their range of effectiveness is limited when conditions change or a new opportunity arises. The lodge may offer a "big fish" trip to some deeper, faster water and the one sinking tip line will not have a fast enough sink rate to get the fly to the fish. What you have, then, is an angler who has spent thousands of dollars to take a dream trip and misses the fishing of a lifetime because a $40 line isn't part of their system!

A more systematic way to acquire lines is based on the type of fishing situations you're most likely to encounter. The goal is to have the lines that will enable you to present your fly from top to bottom and anywhere in between. This approach to buying lines will greatly increase your range of effectiveness and your chances of taking fish in any situation or condition. This is the ultimate "success insurance."

Our Advice: We recommend adding one line at a time and mastering it before adding another to avoid ending up with a lot of lines you may not really need.

The Starter System, for example, would consist of an Ultra² floating line, a Wet Tip® III (Hi-D®) and a Wet Cel® Uniform Sink II. These lines will take care of most needs when fishing moving waters on the surface, and in medium currents and up to eight to 10 feet deep in stillwater. The main limitations of this system are fishing deeper or faster currents.

In lakes, your Uniform Sink II will be too fast and will soon have your fly hung up when the fish are working over weed beds or flats three to five feet deep. On the other extreme, if the fish are deeper than eight to 10 feet or are moving quickly, you just won't be able to reach them fast enough.

To create an Intermediate Angler System that will increase your range of effectiveness, you would add a Wet Tip® IV (Hi-Speed® Hi-D®) and a Wet Cel® Uniform Sink III (Hi-D®). By adding these two faster sink rate lines, you will be able to get deep fast in strong currents or reach quickly moving fish in stillwaters. You'll also be able to explore deep pools in streams and rivers with moderately fast current. (Haven't you always wondered what size fish lurked at the bottom of those dark, deep pools?) Now, you're only limited in very shallow water situations and, when the fish are really deep or moving really fast, like when they're chasing baitfish.

Ultimately, as your ability grows and your interests widen, you may wish to develop an Advanced Angler System. A Wet Cel® Intermediate, a Wet Cel® monocore and a Wet Cel® Uniform Sink V will increase your range at either end of the sinking spectrum. You will be able to fish slowly just below the surface in streams and lakes or head for the bottom fast.

You will now be able to keep your fly just inches below the surface with your Wet Cel® Intermediate's extra slow sink rate. This line is especially helpful in windy conditions when your high-floating line will sail across the surface unnaturally, dragging your fly with it. The Wet Cel® Monocore earns its keep when working the shallows for extra wary fish and is also a must for the saltwater flats. When you need to go deep fast, you will have the fastest full sinking fly line made when you have a Uniform Sink V in your system.

Heartache River

by Mike Dry

"*T*here she is boys," yelled Ron, our pilot and guide, above the grind of engines and lowered flaps as we banked steeply left. We had been flying parallel to the coastline along Alaska's Bristol Bay and, now, as the horizon leveled out, we saw our angling destination for the day.

"Our secret river drains the ocean into that little bay on the right. That's where the fish feed." On our descent into a little lake, we could see the first group from camp making a short hike to the spike camp near the river's edge. Such a stark, barren landscape in the middle of *terra incognito* seemed fitting terrain to cross to find the fish of our dreams.

While Ron lead our party of six, my fishing companion, Howard West, and I lagged behind, slogging along in the spongy tundra, laughing skeptically about the monsters cruising this secret, "no-name" river. The fishing had been poor and the stories we heard at camp about this place seemed like more hype to pick up our spirits. Suddenly, one of the guides from the spike camp came trotting toward us.

"Get these guys on the water, Ron," he said. "The river just came up about 30 minutes ago and one guy already hung a 39-inch rainbow!" Collectively, the whole group caught its breath and fell silent. "OK, boys," said Ron, "Here's the plan." He described a simple strategy: he would walk us up river, dropping off individual anglers at the best pools along the way. Later, one of the other guides would check to see how everyone was doing and, if need be, move us around.

"These steelhead are running up river on a high tide," Ron said. "But they won't be here forever. They'll go back out with the tide. You've got a couple of hours of red-hot fishing. Make 'em count!"

We walked quickly, now, following Ron up river as he dropped off the other anglers at their pools. Then it was just Howard and me.

"Hang a monster!" I shouted as I watched Howard scramble down the steep bank toward the river which looked very full and swift.

As Ron and I walked further upstream, we saw an angler from the other group on the far bank, battling a large fish with a spinning rod. The fisherman had a very uneasy look on his face as the fish made powerful runs and, each time the fish jumped, he look quite surprised. "Stay with him, Jim," Ron yelled. "Just don't horse him." Soon the rainbow was flopping on the bank and, as Jim grabbed it, several long silver fish slid from its mouth.

"Those are baitfish the rainbows are feeding on out in the salt," said Ron. "Look at their stomachs!" I glanced down at the large black fly—one of my own creations freshly tied last night—on the end of my heavy leader. "Don't worry about your fly. These fish will hit anything you put in front of them. You're fine." Ron waved his arm at me and headed upstream.

Soon we were at "my" pool several hundred yards upstream from Jim and Howard, but as I moved into position, I could see they both had fish on. Before Ron had taken two steps back downstream, my fly hit the water! I had tried to stay cool on the walk up, but I was shaking now. Jim's fish had really unsettled me. ("Looks like about eight pounds," Ron had said. "Nice fish but lots bigger in here.") The biggest trout I'd landed anywhere was a little under five pounds and that had seemed enormous on the 7-weight outfit I was using.

Nearly 40 minutes passed without a bump. Meanwhile, every time I looked downriver, it seemed like someone in the group had a fish on during this feeding frenzy of big steelhead. What the hell was I doing wrong? Just as I made another half-hearted cast, John, our other guide, appeared in the Zodiac. "Got that big one, Mike?" he yelled into the wind. "Afraid not. I haven't hooked anything, yet." I was *(continued on page 38)*

With the eight lines listed, you can fish effectively from top to bottom and anywhere in between. Your only limitation with this system is distance because standard fly lines are effective for casts up to about 70 to 80 feet. So, when you are regularly faced with situations requiring casts of 80 feet or more—large rivers or lakes, for example—you may want to create a Mastery Angler System by adding a selection of 30-foot Shooting Taper lines.

You'll need the following shooting tapers (ST) :

- Wet Cel® I
  sink rate range: 1.75-2.50 ips

- Wet Cel® II
  sink rate range: 2.25-3.00 ips

- Wet Cel® (Hi-D®)
  sink rate range: 3.25-4.25 ips

- Wet Cel® Hi-Speed® (Hi-D®)
  sink rate range: 3.75-6.50 ips

- Deep Water Express™
  sink rate range: 7.00-10.00 ips

- Ultra² .029 floating shooting line

What you'll notice is that the shooting taper system nearly duplicates the sink rates of the lines in the Advanced Angler System. Essentially, the shooting tapered lines will increase your casting distance range because the entire weight of a shooting taper is concentrated in a 30-foot section of line rather than the long belly section of the standard weight forward line. The combination of the "pulling power" of the short taper and the low resistance of the small diameter (.029 inches) shooting line creates the potential of casts in excess of 100 feet.

Mastery Angler System is the ultimate line system. For the price of another quality fly rod, you can own a system of lines that will get your fly to any practical depth and cover any piece of water you're likely to encounter. Anywhere. Your investment in lines is a sound one because, even if your fishing demands are heavy, the lines will last for years. But the ultimate return on your investment will be those situations where your lines enabled you to take fish you would have missed without them! That's when the Mastery System pays big dividends.

The greater the variety or the higher

degree of uncertainty about the situations and conditions you'll fish, the more lines you'll need.

(For a complete look at the full range of SA lines, see our catalog at the end of the book.)

Extra Lines, Extra Spools

As you consider your angling needs and the system of lines you plan to build, it will become readily apparent that you will need at least two and possibly several extra spools for the extra lines. Unfortunately, for some anglers, this additional expense has prevented them from owning the lines they need to succeed.

For greatest economy and convenience in handling your line system, we recommend you use a combination of extra spools and the Loop System.

You must first identify the lines you use most frequently and buy extra spools for them. Interchangeable spools loaded with your favorite lines is certainly the easiest, quickest method when using more than one line. And, if you can afford it and you want the instant availability of different lines, extra spools for all your lines is the ideal way to go.

But, if you don't mind giving up some convenience to save a few dollars, the Loop System offers some real advantages. By putting loops on the end of your fly line and backing, such a system allows you to use many fly lines with one spool. The lines you choose for this system should be the ones you use less often but still want to have available.

This way, you can go into the field with frequently used lines already attached to extra reel spools and other lines stored on their plastic fly line spools (ones that

The Loop System

1. *Form a 12" backing loop.*
2. *Make a double overhand knot about 6" from the end of the loop.*
3. *Pull the knot tight and trim the tag end.*
4. *Cut an 8" piece of monofilament. Form 2" loop in the fly line.*
5. *With the 10 lb. mono, make a nail knot about ¹/₂" from the end of the loop.*
6. *Tighten and trim.*
7. *Pass the backing loop through the fly line loop, then pass the backing loop over the fly reel.*
8. *As you tighten the junction it should look like this. . .*
9. *Not like this.*

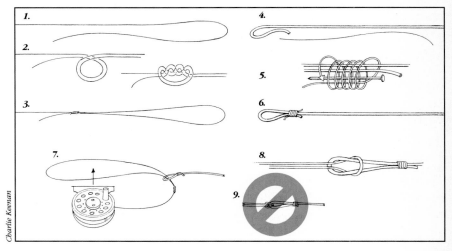

Charlie Keenan

may make your trip by filling a special need) looped and ready to be switched from the plastic fly line spool to your fly reel spool (to keep the plastic spools from separating, glue them together with fly tying cement). This system will also take up less space, an issue that can become very important on those long trips far from the nearest tackle store and extra lines! No matter how thoroughly you plan a trip, it is almost impossible to know about all the conditions you'll face when travelling to new fishing locations.

So make sure the line system you bring gives you a full range of options to cover a variety of angling needs. You'll be amazed at how many lines you can carry with the Loop System and how often one of these lines "saves the day," especially when you're travelling someplace new. Instead of being just another frustrated angler that can't get their fly to the fish, you'll get a special satisfaction looping on the line that puts your fly right where you want it!

Our Advice: Another way to hold down costs is to make sure you buy a quality reel that offers reasonably priced extra spools. Some manufacturers don't do

Heartache River, cont.

totally lost.

John beached the boat and stood nearby, coaching and building up my spirits as I continued to flail the water. With every passing moment that was pulling me toward the end of a day that I had hoped would be the best of angling days but threatened to be the worst, my desperation grew. Nothing worked. Cast after cast without a bump. We moved to another pool, we changed flies, tried casting farther upstream. No fish. The look in John's eyes told me he had given me everything he had to offer and it was not to be. Finally, I asked him to ferry me down to Howard's pool. At least I could watch someone else catch fish and, maybe, learn something.

Almost two hours had passed since we had begun fishing and, as the Zodiac scraped to a landing, I could tell from the glow on Howard's face that his time had been well spent.

"Hey, big guy! Did you get a monster with that fly of yours?" Howard had worked patiently with me at the tying table night after night until I could produce a passable wet fly and he had shared my joy at taking some fish with these flies. But, now, nothing had worked. I explained my dilemma in great detail.

"Can you feel the line bump along the bottom?" Howard asked.

"When the line drifts, I don't feel anything," I answered.

"Let's take a look." Howard put down his rod and examined my outfit. "Do you know what this sink rate is?"

"No," I answered as I handed the rod to Howard, "but the guy at the shop said it was what I needed." Making a short cast, Howard watched the tip sink.

"Looks like a slow sinker," Howard said. "That's the problem. It's just not sinking fast enough in this current to get your fly down on the bottom. That's where the fish are."

I stared hard into the water until my eyes wouldn't focus.

"Hey, listen. I need a break. Why don't you try this?" Howard handed me his rod and sat down on the bank. "It's an 8-weight Wet Tip® IV. It'll sink your fly like a rock!"

Too grateful and excited to refuse the gesture, I grabbed the rod and moved into the edge of the current. I was surprised how quickly the tip sank, as I mended the line with the drift. I felt the line ticking along the bottom for the first time that day.

"Feel the line bumping?" asked Howard. Before I could answer, a fish struck. Not hard but solid. And, in a few moments, I landed a two-pound rainbow. Not one of the giants I pursued, hardly worth a look by Alaskan standards. There was no joy in that fish, no sense of encouragement. I knew the run was over just as surely as I knew why I had not taken fish that afternoon.

Soon, we were all headed back to the lodge, the plane filled with anglers giddy from the day's adventure and the tales they would tell through the wee hours of our last night together in the bush. As the plane floated past the snow-capped peaks now bathed in the glow of the early summer's fading light, I could only see the huge, sea-run rainbows: the biggest fish I had ever seen, fish any man would pay any price to hook and land, holding on the bottom of my pool, waiting for the tide to change for the next run to the sea, their eyes staring cold and empty as my fly passed far above their heads again and again and again. . .

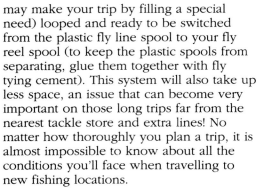

this and it can create a real problem down the road for the angler building a system of lines.

Specialty Lines:
The ultimate in performance

Before long, there's one thing about fly fishing we all realize: you cannot predict where your interests and fortunes will take you. The man or woman totally devoted to the subtleties of spring creek trout fishing will one day find themselves on a bonefish flat in Belize, a Pacific steelhead river or some other exciting destination.

When a passion for new challenges develops, the angler dedicated to the advantages of the right tackle will turn to the higher performance of specialty lines. These fly fishers have already discovered from experience that the more specialized the situation, the more specialized their tackle system should be. An angler newly-hooked on catching "bones," the silver bullets of the flats, for example, will turn to specialty lines to get the extra edge these lines provide and experience the ultimate in presentation performance.

There's a whole new generation of lines because of the increased interest in specializing on a specific species. The new lines are really a mirror of our customers' needs. With the SA team as well as field testers and customers travelling to the Four Corners of the World in pursuit of new experiences, we have developed lines with specific performance qualities to help them master the situations and conditions they encounter. It is no longer an exotic rarity to see magazine photos of fly fishers with everything from monster steelhead to huge billfish, tuna and tarpon. And the desire for such experiences spreads rapidly each year. (Picture yourself hooked to a 200-pound tarpon, over seven feet in length with a 44-inch girth. It's enough to send anyone to the nearest travel agent!)

The Scientific Anglers team has shared the excitement of exploring new angling frontiers from Belize to New Zealand and is proud to have been part of the process for the last 35 years. Our lab people are constantly developing new experimental lines. Then, our worldwide field testing organization reports its evaluation of prototype lines that influence the final design of the lines that end up on your reels. The dynamics of this process has produced the current generation of specialty lines and will lead to the development of whatever lines are

necessary to meet the needs of this new breed of angler.

So far, lines for specific species like bass, tarpon, bonefish and steelhead have emerged from 3M/Scientific Anglers laboratories. These lines are designed to increase your effectiveness beyond the traditional lines that may be a part of your system. Owning these lines is a way to fine tune your fly line system and give you performance benefits you'll appreciate when angling for new species in their unique environments.

Although the standard floating line tapers are unsurpassed for handling a broad range of typical situations and conditions, they do have limitations. For example, bass fly fishers often concentrate on casting to structure and edges like sunken trees or lily pad beds. Once the cast is retrieved 10 feet or so from the "hot spot," the probability of a strike is low it's time to cast again. With a standard WF line, this means making numerous false casts in order to work the long belly of the line back out of the guides before the next cast can be shot back to the target. In short, too much time is spent with your fly in the air and not on the water.

We solved this problem by producing a line that had a shorter belly and short front and rear tapers. And we called it the Bass Bug Taper. With it, fly rodders found they

Steelhead Tapers

A longer tip section (13 feet) lets you fish a certain depth longer than shorter tips that plane up in the current. A new faster sink rate makes this the perfect line for getting deeper faster in moving water. The improved taper blends the sinking portion to the floating line over a greater distance minimizing the "hinging" that makes casting sinking tip lines more difficult.

Wet Tip® III
  13 foot WF 7-10 F/S
  Tip color: Greenish Black
Wet Tip® IV
  13 foot WF 7-10 F/S
  Tip color: Gray
Wet Tip® V
  13 foot WF 7-10 F/S
  Tip color: Black

High-performance lines for specialized situations and conditions.

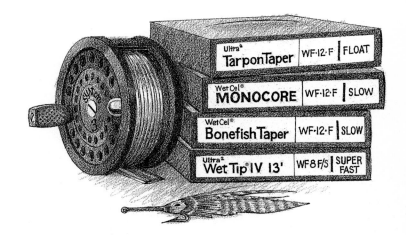

could shoot a cast 50 to 60 feet with ease, retrieve it and, then, pick the line off the water and shoot it to the next target with *one* false cast. As a result, an average caster can now cover about twice the amount of water with the BBT than with the standard WF line. In addition to this greater productivity, fly fishers using this new line also find it's much easier to cast large, more air-resistant flies because of the shorter, more concentrated weight of the belly.

Long ago, this specialty line also found its way into the hands of adventurers to saltwater. They also liked the shorter taper design because they could get off a cast far more quickly, a real advantage on the flats for fast-cruising bonefish and tarpon. Yet, they couldn't always get the distance they needed because the extreme heat of the tropical climate caused standard lines to become too soft.

The solution to this "wilting" effect came during the filming of our *Fly Rodding for Tarpon* series. At the insistence of our on-camera expert, Billy Pate, we tried coating a braided monofilament material he had used very successfully as a shooting line. The results were spectacular: not only were the new lines stiffer, the braided core gave the small diameter running line a textured finish. Together, these two features greatly increased shootability, making it possible for a good caster to throw the full 100 feet of line with only one or two false casts!

And when the wind starts howling and your floating line becomes difficult to cast or gets blown around on the water, you can switch to the sinking version that will penetrate the wind because of its overall smaller diameter. For example, the diameter of the belly for a 7-weight floating Bonefish Taper line is .055 of an inch, while it is only .033 of an inch for the slow sinking (1.40 to 1.80 ips) model. That's 40 percent less surface area. It also has a slightly smaller, stiffer running line with a slight texture so you can cast farther.

No wonder that in just a few years our Bonefish and Tarpon Taper lines have become the first choice of flats anglers around the world.

Fly Fishing for Pacific Steelhead, Advanced Fly Fishing for Pacific Steelhead, Fly Fishing for Trophy Steelhead and Catching More Steelhead

These four tapes about the ultimate West Coast fly fishing challenge, catching steelhead on the fly, feature noted steelheading authorities, Lani Waller, in three tapes and Jim Teeny in a fourth. Even though you may have fished extensively for rainbow trout, steelhead are a whole different breed.

You'll need to use totally different tackle and angling techniques to successfully fish for steelhead. These are big fish. Most anglers are a little stunned when they discover their size and power. When they hook one of these bruisers that are in the 10 to 15 pound range but can run over 20, they find out in a hurry if they've got the right tackle!

If you want to get serious about steelhead—particularly if you're going to take a Big Trip—this series on steelhead is great insurance to assure you of success.

Fishing for Pacific Steelhead demonstrates all the fundamental concepts and techniques you'll need to enjoy consistent angling success for these magnificent fish. Steelhead behavior, where and why they hold in different parts of the river, what tackle to use and how to present your fly.

Advanced Fly Fishing for Pacific Steelhead builds on the fundatmentals of the first tape and teaches you the skills you'll need to catch steelhead under the most

In pursuit of angling pleasures, you may find yourself fishing the evening rise on exotic rivers like the Malleo in Argentina.

Valentine Atkinson

challenging of situations. You'll learn about the things that influence steelhead behavior, proven methods for finding and hooking fish in deep water and how to fish the classic steelhead presentation methods.

Fly Fishing for Trophy Steelhead takes you on an adventure to the wilds of British Columbia in pursuit of trophy steelhead. Lani demonstrates his favorite dry-fly techniques, how to approach each new piece of water with a specific plan, how to adapt classic steelhead presentation methods to trophy situations and how to handle 20-pound steelhead in heavy water.

Catching More Steelhead Fishing to sighted fish is the ultimate thrill in fly fishing for steelhead and the cornerstone of Jim Teeny's highly effective, exciting and unusual methods. You'll learn his unique techniques for spotting, stalking and hooking steelhead under the most challenging situations. You'll also learn how to effectively "time the run" and choose a river plus select the best equipment to make the proper presentation. These techniques will work for you wherever you fish for steelhead.

With a taper design similar to the Bonefish and Tarpon Tapers, our Monocore line is truly unique: it has a clear, single strand of monofilament core and coating that makes it almost invisible. Perfect for those bright days on the flats when the fish are super spooky, this line has been nicknamed the "slime line" because of its slippery feel when wet. . . a real bonus when you need to shoot line. But, as so often happens, anglers that have used the Monocore successfully on the flats have taken advantage of its characteristics when fishing for other species on other waters. Bass and trout anglers, for example, have found it an ideal solution for those lakes that are exceptionally clear.

The most recent addition to our Ultra ^{2} specialty floating line family is the Steelhead Taper, a line with an interesting evolutionary story of its own. Every August, when the flats get too hot for comfort, many of our saltwater field testers head to the cool steelhead rivers of the Northwest. After a season of testing Bonefish Taper lines, they headed north across the country with their favorite flats lines. The testers reported they loved the way the line shot, but found the shorter belly was more difficult to mend, a real problem in getting the long, controlled drifts steelheaders need.

So our plant, which includes a couple of wild-eyed, steelhead fanatics, went to work on developing a special floating Steelhead Taper line. They combined a braided monofilament core material—similar to what had worked so well in the Bonefish Taper lines—with a radically different taper design. And the results surpassed everyone's expectations. What makes the new design so exciting is that its longer belly and extra-long rear taper make mending a dream, even at long distances. And the stiffer, smaller diameter running line makes very long casts—80 to 90 feet—easy for a good caster. In fact, if you're not careful, you'll find yourself doing more casting with the Steelhead Taper line than fishing!

If you've graduated from inland rainbows to their giant ocean-fed cousins, our 13-foot Sinking Tip Steelhead Taper series will help you. They keep your fly at the right level longer and make casting all day long a lot easier. Available in three sink rates, including a new ultra-fast sink rate (Wet Tip V with a sink rate of 5.5-6.5 ips). It's the fastest sinking tip line made. All three lines are available in 90-foot lengths to accommodate the long cast you will often need to make on steelhead rivers.

The Steelhead Trout
This is a classic. Originally issued in 1971, Trey Combs draws on a lifetime fascination with these great fish to describe their migrating habits, range from California to Alaska and the most effective fly patterns. Of particular interest is his documentation of both fly and drift fishing techniques and a 135 steelhead pattern fly directory. If you're not sure you want to fish for steelhead, this book will definitely change your mind and have you planning your first trip. Opens up the whole fascinating world of steelhead fishing and tells you the best way to enter.

Anatomy of a Fly Reel
There is no piece of fly tackle that is so often neglected when putting together a fly fishing system. It is amazing how often an angler will devote huge amounts of time researching and testing fly rods before spending large amounts of money only to grab the nearest reel for that rod!

This attitude toward reels probably comes from the old maxim that says, "A reel is only a place to store line." This still rings

Anglers that have used the Monocore successfully on the flats have taken advantage of its characteristics when fishing for other species.

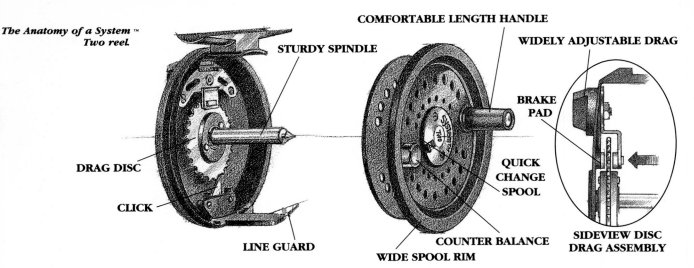

The Anatomy of a System ™ Two reel.

COMFORTABLE LENGTH HANDLE

STURDY SPINDLE

WIDELY ADJUSTABLE DRAG

BRAKE PAD

DRAG DISC

QUICK CHANGE SPOOL

CLICK

LINE GUARD

COUNTER BALANCE

SIDEVIEW DISC DRAG ASSEMBLY

WIDE SPOOL RIM

true for some fly fishers who are content to cast for panfish a few times each summer or try for small trout. But, for the angler who is committed to exploring fly fishing's many opportunities and wants to enjoy these experiences to the fullest, the use of a fine reel can be one of fly fishing's great joys.

Many anglers start fly fishing with an inexpensive reel. It seems to work just fine for the first kinds of fishing they do for smaller species and smaller fish they tend to catch. But, the first time they hook a fish of major proportions, they discover some serious limitations of their reel. When that big fish takes out line in a hurry and the line comes off in jerky bursts—maybe even breaking the leader—they have a clear understanding of how important it is to use a quality reel. Or, the line may race wildly, creating a backlash that jams the spool and causes the leader to break. One experience like this is usually enough to send any angler on a hurried search for a quality reel!

For some anglers, these problems with a reel never happen. But, if you start fishing for big, fast or mean fish—steelhead, salmon and bonefish, tarpon or 'cuda—without a high performance reel, your chances of success are greatly reduced and, in some situations, almost zero. The reason is that you beat a big fish with the drag system of your reel. While it's true that an angler often needs a strong back and powerful rod when tangling with large species, it's the drag that wears down the fish and brings it to hand. The smooth, constant pressure of a powerful drag will win the day for you.

There are a number of advantages to consider when purchasing a reel for your fly fishing system.

Of great importance—and often over-looked—is using a reel that matches the rest of the system. Like rods, the best reels are designed for specific line weights. Typically, a reel will fit a system designed for two or three different weights (SA's System™ Two reels, for example, are made in four sizes to fit line weights 67, 78, 89 & 1011). The reason for this is that the correct reel has the right backing capacity for the species you're after and the correct weight to balance your rod. You'll really appreciate a balanced system after a long day on the water—especially using systems at the power end of the line weight spectrum. (Incidentally, many anglers who complain about their rod action discover the problem is a reel that is too heavy or too light.)

Another feature that can be critical—especially when you're attached to fish of real size and power—is *durability*. It's really incredible how much abuse reels take over the years. Banged on rocks, dropped in the bottom of a boat, squished in mud and sand—you name it, it will happen to your reel. Usually, when you're busy with other things. And there is no agent more destructive than saltwater which will quickly corrode any reel that does not have parts made of stainless steel or is not protected by special finishes.

Over time, such things will cause reels that are poorly designed or made of inexpensive materials to fail just when you need them most, usually when you've hooked the fish of the trip or a lifetime! And, as you might expect, the places reels fail most often are the frame and the drag. Typically, these are reels that are designed to be lightweight at the expense of durability. So, for some extra insurance, invest in the best quality reel you can afford, one of proven design and with a history of enduring normal abuse active anglers tend to give them. Kept in good working order, such reels should last for decades.

Just like fly lines, reels are also designed with specific tasks in mind and have limitations that are broader but no less important for you to know when choosing the right tackle. Knowing the "specs" on reels you own or plan to buy can be an important influence on your decisions about the right system to use. Many of today's anglers face a wide variety of fly fishing situations which place greater demand than ever on the fly reel. Just as no one fly reel meets all conditions, no one reel can do it all.

Leaders & Tippets: *The weakest link*

Making sure you have a good variety of high-performance leaders and tippets and matching them to your fly line is important to effective casting. The right leader/tippet system for individual situations and conditions has a greater influence on getting a natural drift of your fly than many anglers suspect. You will need to keep a number of things in mind when choosing the best leaders and tippets for the fishing you do.

Our Advice: Don't trust leaders and especially tippets over one or two seasons. Mono loses its strength with age, while sunlight and heat accelerate the aging process. Be sure to store your leader/tippet material in dark cool place.

Leaders for Floating Lines

Whether you buy or tie your own, you should consider using relatively long leaders—9-foot is a good length—on floating fly lines for greater depth versatility and presentation capabilities. In addition to fishing surface flies, a longer leader will give you the option of fishing weighted flies below the surface when the water depth is in the three to five foot range, depending on what technique you're using. The other advantage of longer leaders is you'll spook fewer fish and get a more natural float of your fly. Particularly when combined with a long, soft tippet, long leaders will help you take the more difficult fish whatever the species, no matter how clear the water.

Choosing a high performance leader is an inexpensive but important decision to make. The problem is determining quality. Features like stretch, breaking strength and taper are all but impossible to evaluate any place but on the water. Then you may pay

a price to learn about the flaws in your leader!

Relationship Between Tippet Size and Hook Size	
Tippet Diameter (inches)	Hook Size
.011 (0X)	1/0 - 4
.010 (1X)	4 - 8
.009 (2X)	6 - 10
.008 (3X)	10 - 14
.007 (4X)	12 - 16
.006 (5X)	14 - 22
.005 (6X)	16 - 24
.004 (7X)	18 - 28
.003 (8X)	18 - 28

You'll want high quality monofilament that resists all the wear and tear that will cause a leader to fail when you least expect it. You'll want a leader designed to turn over smoothly in different conditions without forcing it. You'll want a leader supple enough to let your fly float naturally, particularly when you fish on top. As a general rule, price is a good indicator of performance. The better leaders simply cost more because of the expense of materials and production. Poorly designed leaders won't turn over well and will often break without apparent cause.

Sinking Line Leaders

When fishing below the surface with a sinking tip or full sinking line, you'll need a leader that's much shorter with less taper than the floating line leaders. Usually, four to six feet is fine. Again, length will be determined by the angling situation you face—size of fly, water clarity, wind, etc.—but keep in mind two things: if the leader gets too short, it will be harder to cast and, in clear water, it will spook fish more easily.

The other important thing to consider when choosing your leader length is the planing effect that occurs with all sinking lines during retrieval. Depending on how fast you retrieve and, in moving water, the current speed, your line and leader will plane and drag your fly along with it. How much depends on the length of your leader.

Remember: during your retrieve, the shorter the leader, the closer your fly will be to the depth of your fly line.

Leader Systems

Many anglers forget: you must match your leader system to the fly you're casting.

That's why it is so important to understand what individual leaders and tippets can do. Like all the other components of your fly fishing system, individual leader systems have their limitations, too, and your correct selection of the right system is no less important to your angling success. The best strategy is to make sure you have a wide range of tippets with you and take the time to tune your leader system when you change flies. This is mostly a matter of choosing a tippet of the right length and diameter for the fly you're using. Remember: any formula for matching tippet to fly is only a guideline. Other factors like the wind resistance or the weight of the fly are important as well as the situation and conditions.

The standard leader has been designed to cast small to standard size flies, but with larger, wind-resistant flies, a leader with a heavy butt section is a much better choice. With sufficient line speed, the additional mass of the butt section will help you turnover the bigger flies more easily. Just as you would not use a 5-weight system to cast bass bugs, you wouldn't use the same standard leaders designed for a 5-weight system to cast big flies.

Strength is Not Everything

You may have read about new high-tech leaders made out of "miracle" mono that claim to have a breaking strength far greater than other leaders of the same diameter. The idea is you can fool and land fish with much smaller tippets because they have greater strength than other leaders of the same diameter.

To achieve these higher breaking strength to diameter ratios, the new leaders sacrifice other qualities that make a high performance leader. One important trade-off is the loss of stretch that occurs in the manufacturing process of drawing out the monofilament as the leader is being formed to increase its strength. Stretch in a leader helps absorb sudden shocks such as hook-setting or when a fish bolts. It also controls memory, the cause of those annoying coils that can create presentation problems. Another weakness of the "miracle strength" leaders is their lack of resistance to abrasion which makes them much more susceptible to small nicks from rocks or teeth that can cause a leader to break under light stress.

Guides are invaluable, especially when fishing foreign waters.

Our customers tell us these are poor trade-offs and prefer our more balanced approach to leader design and construction. In addition to wanting a leader that will stretch and hold up to wear and tear, they want one that is made of materials that do not readily absorb water, a feature that will assure you of consistent line and knot strength that reduces the chance of fish break-offs.

A high-performance leader should also be tapered in "steps" like expensive hand-tied leaders so it will turn your fly over and improve your presentation. And, finally, make sure the leaders you buy are manufactured in a variety of strengths and lengths so you can match your leader to your fishing.

Knots

There is probably no other aspect of fly fishing that has caused more unnecessary irritation and anguish than knots.

One problem is with knots infrequently tied. Because we tie them so often, we get pretty comfortable tying flies to tippets or adding tippets to leaders. But, when it comes to the knots we use to put together all the pieces of your system—backing, line and leader—it's a different matter. It's one thing to do this at home with a book of knots nearby and quite another in the field when fish are feeding all around you and

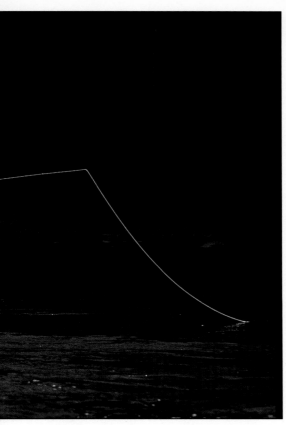

*Guide Joe Howells unlocking the mysteries of the
North Umpqua for a visiting angler.*

there's a break in your system with no knot diagrams in sight! In time, you'll learn to tie all the important knots wherever you are, but until then, we suggest you carry a small booklet with diagrams for those field emergencies. (SA's *Pocket Guide* that comes in every fly line box has these illustrations)

Another problem is the knot that fails when battling a fish, most typically the biggest fish of the trip or, sometimes, the fish of a lifetime. Usually, this occurs at the tippet or fly. That's why it's so important to be able to tie every knot very easily and, regardless of the excitement of the moment, to do so with care and precision. Many a fish has been lost and hearts broken because an angler added tippet material or tied on a new fly too hastily. Whatever knots you learn, learn to tie them well every time. All too often the problem is simply one of wear and tear that weakens the knot. Repeated casting and playing of fish will stress the very best of materials to a breaking point.

Our Advice: Check knots often and don't hesitate to cut off old knots and re-tie them. Be sure to re-tie your fly every couple of hours or after catching a few fish.

The most typical difficulty is one of facility. You must be able to tie frequently used knots quickly and correctly under all kinds of conditions. And this takes practice. There is no point in trying to use a blood knot to connect tippets if you cannot tie it in smaller tippet sizes. That's why it's important to practice your knots with the actual materials you'll be using on the water. If you do not have the dexterity to tie it or the patience to practice it, a double surgeon's knot may be a better choice for you. So make sure you don't waste valuable time on the water or, worse, lose a good fish because of tying problems. And one other thing: if you don't see the knots like you used to, use glasses. They will help enormously, especially in low light conditions. There are lots of great products on the market that combine sunglasses and magnifying glasses, eliminating the inconvenience of using two different kinds of glasses.

Once you've mastered the basic knots for the angling you do, don't stop there. Read up on new knots that you may want to use for special circumstances and learn how to tie them as well. A Duncan Loop, for example, is a great knot because it gives your fly more action and lets it track in the water more independent of the tippet. Sometimes, this will give your fly an added naturalness that will cause strikes you wouldn't get if the fly were attached with a clinch knot. On the other hand, snelling your tarpon flies onto your shock tippet will also improve your angling success because snelled hooks track true with the hook down for better striking. So keep looking for new knots to learn and enjoy the edge you'll have when fishing certain situations. Remember: Your leader system is only as good as the knots that hold it together. Make sure they're done right. Every time.

We've taken a pretty detailed look at the tackle that you'll need to select for your fly fishing systems. With a good sense of what each piece can do in a given situation, you should be able to make the right choices for whatever angling you face. Now, we'd like to take a look at the great variety of ways to use this equipment that will dramatically increase your angling success.

Casting and Presentation Skills: Getting Your Fly to the Fish

Casting is the foundation skill of all the presentation techniques needed to be a successful fly fisher. Presentation really describes two related but different skills:

You must match your leader system to the fly you're casting getting your fly to where the fish are located and, then, getting your fly to appear natural to the fish. In this section, we'll describe the main variety of casting techniques you must learn to accomplish these objectives.

One way to learn these skills is at a fly fishing school. Today, there are many schools offered all over the country, usually in some very nice fishing spots where you can practice what you learn. Even if you have the added expense of driving some distance, a school can be a great weekend fishing vacation. An exciting way to learn, the schools offer one-on-one instruction from teaching professionals who can really accelerate your progress in a short time. Many anglers meet interesting new friends and come back for refresher courses at future dates. The one big drawback with schools, though, is you can't learn it all in just one session.

Valentine Atkinson

Another alternative yet complementary way to improve your fly casting is with a quality instructional video. Let's face it: there is a lot of new stuff to learn about casting, especially the advanced techniques, and, no matter how gifted you are, no one picks up everything in a weekend. That's the beauty of videotapes. Watching professional instructors take you step-by-step through the whole process, you can work on each step at your own pace when it's convenient. Instead of waiting until your instructor holds another school so you can get help, you can cue your tape to the techniques you need to learn now. Researchers have discovered that for the most effective learning you must be able to visualize what you need to do. And, by owning a videotape, you will always have the visualization you need to learn at your fingertips. The camera acts as the eyes of the expert, focusing your attention on the essentials of each instructional step. The availability of these tapes is one of the most revolutionary aids to fly casting in the history of the sport. If you can, be sure and take advantage of some good ones.

But all the best information in the world won't make you a good flycaster unless you practice. The fact is you need to be able to make the right cast in the right situation. When you have to double-haul your fly to a cruising fish that may pass your way only once, you're out of luck if you can only do it on your front lawn after several practice casts! These techniques need to become second nature, something you can do without even thinking about them. That leaves you free to focus on the fish, not the cast. Keep one thing in mind: the best fly fishers are absolutely "psycho" when it comes to casting techniques. That's because they know first hand it pays off in angling success.

Fly Fishing Made Easy

You'll learn to enjoy this sport of fly fishing faster than you ever thought possible. Whether you're after bass, trout or panfish, your fly fishing instructor, Bob Guard, prepares you with these easy steps: select a balanced system of equipment for whatever fishing you choose; assemble your system the right way, the first time; present your fly to the fish with basic casting techniques.

You'll also get an introduction to the Scientific Anglers "Formula for Success" that will help you catch fish in almost any situation. Location. By learning the basics of fish behavior and their feeding habits, you'll be able to locate your favorite speicies wherever you fish. Behavior. By understanding feeding habits and how best to imitate that food, you'll be able to choose the right flies. Presentation. By learning the basic casting techniques, you'll be able to make effective presentations of whatever flies you use.

This is the tape that will teach you all the basics of fly fishing without any frustration. You can progress, step-by-step, at your own pace and develop a solid foundation that will prepare you to travel down the road to fly fishing mastery.

Basic Fly Casting

The first hurdle to overcome in becoming a master trout angler is developing a solid foundation of casting ability. Doug Swisher shows you how to develop your casting skill through his uniquely easy-to-learn technique. You'll learn: why casting works, how to train your mind and muscles to make smooth, controlled casts, how to perfect the basic casting stroke, the principle of loop control, how to make straight line casts and shoot line for distance, the slack line cast and how to recognize your casting mistakes and correct them. The fastest way to learn fly casting, these methods will eliminate frustration and let you spend your time catching fish.

Advanced Fly Casting

Doug Swisher shows the experienced caster how to fish the "impossible" places and helps you make the transition from good caster to master fly fisher.

He reviews the basic casting principles, shows you advanced techniques for getting longer drag-free drifts, increases the accuracy of your slack line casts, teaches you to make accurate curve casts, demonstrates how to "fish the clock," so you can make drag-free presentations to every angle without changing position and how to increase your casting range with the double haul cast. With these skills, you'll be able to fish effectively in every fishing situation.

There's no contest. This is the one tape that will have the greatest impact on your fly fishing success. Whatever the level of your presentation skills, you will learn many techniques that will improve them and help you get your fly in places you thought were impossible to reach. With the kind of successes you'll have after watching this tape, you'll find yourself playing it over and over again to learn new things that will accelerate your presentation skills.

Whatever the source of instruction, the basic cast you must first perfect is the straight line cast. It is the foundation of all the other casting techniques you need to learn. What this means is developing a casting stroke that will allow you to control your line. While there is a certain degree of individuality in casting strokes, all good fly casters are able to keep the line level whether the casting plane is level, up or down. They also have the ability to control the size of the casting loop from very tight to very open.

Once you master these basic skills, you'll need to build off them to improve the quality and versatility of your presentations.

As you work on developing your casting skills, there are three objectives to keep in mind. You need to become accurate so you can put your fly in the target zone which can vary greatly in size and distance. It may be a school of fish feeding on baitfish 80 feet away or a single large trout sipping tiny insects in two square inches of the surface film. You also need to be able to put your fly to the right feeding level anywhere from the top to the bottom or anywhere in between in all kinds of situations and conditions like fast currents and high winds. And, finally, once your fly is at the right feeding level, you must be able to get a natural drift of your fly on the surface or the right action below the surface that causes the fish to strike.

Most of us need little encouragement to work on casting a long line or trying to hit a target. Like hitting a golf ball a long way, it's something that's satisfying in itself. It's also a skill that shows up well on a crowded piece of water or at a casting school. Getting the fly to the fish's depth, while difficult, is more a matter of having the right lines and knowing their range of effectiveness and limitations. Many anglers can acquire this knowledge without much difficulty. But, what really separates the master anglers from everyone else is getting a natural presentation of their fly. This is where physical skills of hand-eye coordination and timing need to be developed to a high degree. And the pay off? You'll catch far more fish and much bigger fish.

You may, for example, locate a monster trout of legendary proportions and select a fly that imitates what he's eating yet still fail to get the fish to take because of an unnatural presentation. All too often this is exactly what happens to good fly fishers who think they've failed because of poor fly selection or casting skill. What you really needed was likely one or two more seconds of drag-free float over a wary fish. And how do you get it? By learning to feed, mend or strip line so the fly drifts naturally for longer amounts of time. Once you see the results such presentation skills produce, it will be one of the most exciting things you've learned about fly fishing and you'll want to learn more. You'll never have to worry about motivation for practice again!

Almost every angler would like to be

SCIENTIFIC ANGLERS

able to cast farther than they can right now. Sometimes, they even want to do this for the right reasons! Usually, we are motivated to develop distance because of the moment that occurs on almost every fishing trip: you've solved the riddle—fish are coming to your fly on a steady basis—and you have a chance at a really good fish but you can't quite get your fly far enough to reach it! (Sorry. Close doesn't count in fly fishing either!) So often, a little more line will help you take that fish. This is nothing a little

double-haul wouldn't fix in a hurry. This casting technique, which does take some timing and practice to do well, is really essential to angling success for almost every species, especially fish in the salt. The more accurate, the better and, if you plan to fish saltwater, add quicker!

The single most important aspects of presentation for stream fly fishers is getting a natural drift of your fly. That's why drag is the greatest presentation problem you'll face on the stream and where major

Camcorder and Casting

A recent addition to the video revolution is the camcorder, an amazing piece of equipment that enables us to point and shoot anything that strikes our fancy and immediately play it back on our television set. Sales of these little hand-held cameras have skyrocketed as they have found useful niches in the corners of all our lives.

Including the fly fisher who seeks to improve his or her casting skills.

Whether you go to a fly fishing school or learn on your own, you can benefit greatly by using a camcorder because developing presentation skills is a long-term process that this little machine can dramatically shorten.

If you've been to a fly fishing school, you know one of its great advantages is having a trained professional help you with your casting. This individual first demonstrates the basics, then, while you try to imitate those moves, the instructor comes around to help you do it right. Step by step, you learn the mechanics of casting this way until you have a solid foundation and can make specific casts. Typically, when you get back home or onto the water, you run into problems which are difficult, if not impossible, to correct on your own. Why? Because the instructor is back at school teaching some new students and you can't see what you're doing wrong.

This is where the camcorder comes in and the power of video can help.

The camcorder works best with a good videotape on casting, one that will take you through the different casts you want to learn in a progressive process. By that, we mean you practice the individual parts until you can put them all together in a cast you

can repeat consistently under any condition you might face.

What you are trying to do is duplicate what you see in the instructional video and, to do that, you'll need to look at how your casting matches the video instructor's casting. By setting up the video tape inside and your camcorder on a tripod outside, you can watch a portion of the tape you want to duplicate, then film your efforts with the camcorder. Then compare the two.

The big surprise is how easily you will be able to see your mistakes when comparing your casts with those of the video instructor. (Your deviation from the correct form will be much easier to see if you film yourself at the same angle as the instructor in the tape.) And a good tape will also tell you how to correct your mistakes like a "tailing" loop or a loop that's too wide. These corrective measures will be more easily understood when you look at your cast and can understand Why it isn't working properly.

This all sounds very simple and it is. The important thing is that, together, these tools can help you become a better caster in a short amount of time. Best of all, when you do have problems (and everyone does), you'll know the "Why" behind those difficulties and can correct them yourself.

So, if you own a camcorder, buy a casting video that matches your skill level and give them both a try. Looking at your fly casting on tape is like listening to your voice on a tape recorder: it will give you a whole new perspective on yourself. And, combined with the casting tape, you'll be able to develop your presentation skills very rapidly and improve your angling success.

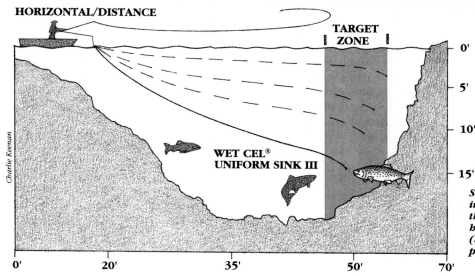

Skilled presentation includes the ability to hit the Target Zone in the horizontal plane (accuracy) and vertical plane (depth).

frustrations begin. Whether fishing on top or below, controlling the line so it does not interfere with the way your fly moves in the water is essential to angling success. The key to successful drifts is getting slack in the line in the right places and keeping it there till a fish strikes or the fly drifts through the target zone. Good instruction will teach you to make slack line casts and, once your line hits the water, manipulate the line by mending, feeding or stripping to maintain the proper amount of slack and get longer floats regardless of water speed or direction. These techniques are not difficult to learn and will have an enormous influence on your angling success.

The other important objective of presentation is to put your fly wherever fish are, not just the easy, obvious locations. Since it is usually true that the best fish are in the worst spots to put your fly, the ability to put your fly where you want it and get a natural float or drift will enable you to take more fish and bigger fish. It will help you tremendously to think about presentation in two planes. When casting horizontally, you are concerned about the casting accuracy and distance required to put your fly in your target area. This is fine for surface presentations. But, when fishing below the surface, you move into the vertical perspective as you use sinking lines that get your fly to a specific depth and keep it there as long as possible.

As your skills in locating fish increase, you'll find the demand for these more advanced casts increases, too. The goal here is to learn the various specialty casts like the reach, curve and reach/curve and which will let you fish locations most anglers pass up. Nothing is more frustrating

to the angler than to locate a great fish and either spook it with a poor cast or not know the cast that will reach it. The ability to put your fly exactly where you want it will open up a whole new area of fly fishing for you.

Finally, you must learn to present your fly in special situations and conditions where you will have to adapt your casting. By "situations," we mean a spot where you have to use a rollcast to avoid the brush right behind you or where you must cover a wide run with a reach cast to fish the far bank. By "conditions," we mean overcoming nature's variables like strong winds by controlling line speed and loop size.

Many fly fishers are totally frustrated when they come from an area where the wind is insignificant to places like the saltwater flats or Western waters where fishing in high winds is a way of life. It is equally maddening to find your casting range or accuracy is not equal to the demands of the fish you pursue. That's why it's important to learn how to deal with these conditions before you face them. Learning to cast sidearm, throwing a tight, dart-like loop, double-hauling to get maximum line speed—techniques like these will again pay off for you with fish that would not otherwise be caught.

As a guide for your own development, you can look at these techniques in this chart. And the best way to learn them is with a videotape from SA's Mastery Series called *Advanced Fly Casting* featuring Doug Swisher. If you're really serious about improving your casting skills and you only buy one video, this is it. Your enjoyment of casting and fly fishing will increase ten-fold if you can learn to do half the things this

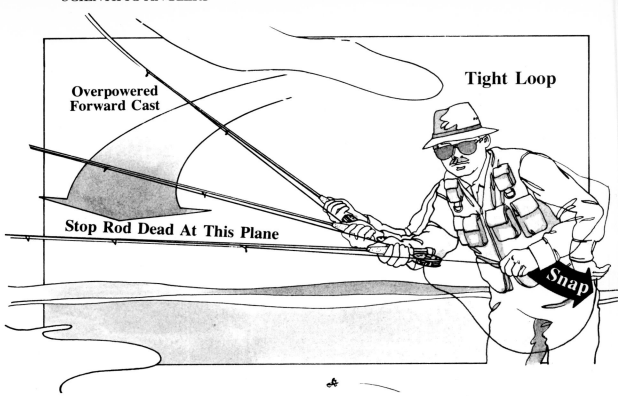

tape will teach you. You'll catch more fish and have more fun from this $50 than any other investment you'll make in fly fishing.

Basic
Skill
Level

• Straight Line cast

• Slack Line cast

• Add mending

• Add reach

• Add feeding

• Add curve

• Double-haul

Mastery • Add specialty casts

The Straight Line and Slack Line casts will enable you to fish effectively in many situations. But learning additional casting techniques is also very important. With them, you'll be able to add additional Drag-Free float time to your cast and put your fly in those "impossible" places.

Essence of Presentation

Looking back on all the presentation techniques available to the fly fisher, it may seem like a lot to learn. But keep two things in mind. Developing these skills is a progressive progress and you can have lots of fun travelling at your own pace. There are no tests, there are no grades. (Besides, it wouldn't be nearly as much fun if you learned it all too quickly!) And, like the other parts of the Formula for Success, the experiences you'll have in the field will only reinforce what you've put into this part of the Formula. Just concentrate on making good presentations in tough situations and you'll enjoy your fishing much more. Even if you don't always get a strike, there's real satisfaction in performing the technique well.

But there is one important thing to remember about these techniques: they have all been developed so you will have effective ways to get your fly to fish wherever they're feeding.

Ideally, the best fly fishers locate fish and determine what they're feeding on, then—whether the fish are on the bottom, on top or anywhere in between in moving water or still—they decide how to present

If you're having difficulty locating any of our products, call us. We'll put you in touch with the nearest Scientific Anglers dealer.

1-800-525-6290

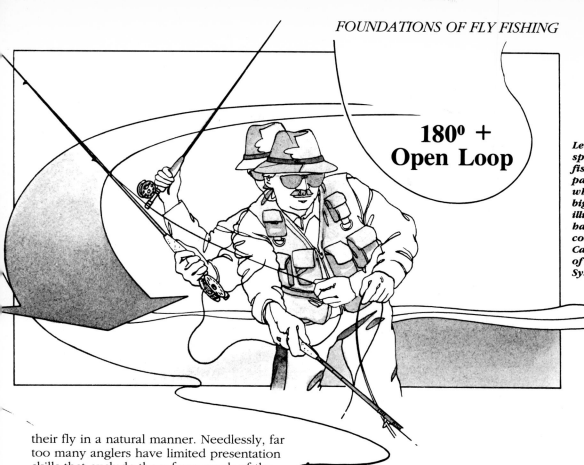

180⁰ +
Open Loop

Learning the various specialty casts will let you fish locations most anglers pass up, usually the spots where you'll find the biggest fish. (These illustrations are from the hardbound guidebook that comes with the Advanced Casting videotapes as part of the Mastery Learning System series.)

their fly in a natural manner. Needlessly, far too many anglers have limited presentation skills that exclude them from much of the best fishing and biggest fish. Even when they take a "dream trip" to some remote place where wild fish are eager to strike and they use a guide to locate fish and select flies for them, these anglers are frequently unable to catch fish because they lack proper presentation skills. They are stuck on using only a floating line and just one or two presentation casts—the basic straight line or slack line, for example.

So, if you are committed to becoming an accomplished angler, the one thing that will most increase your angling success is to improve your presentation skills. This is where the Formula for Success all comes together: equipment, knowledge and skill. That means using a system of tackle that will handle the fishing situations and conditions you face and knowing the limitations of each component of that system so you can select the right tackle that can effectively deliver your fly to the fish you're after. It also means learning many new casting techniques to improve the quality of your presentation.

All of this will take some time. The reading you do, the tackle you purchase and the time you practice your casting will give you more and more pleasure. And you will experience the very special thrills that

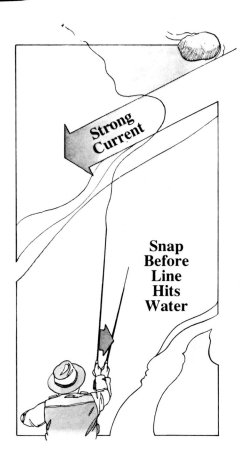

Strong Current

Snap Before Line Hits Water

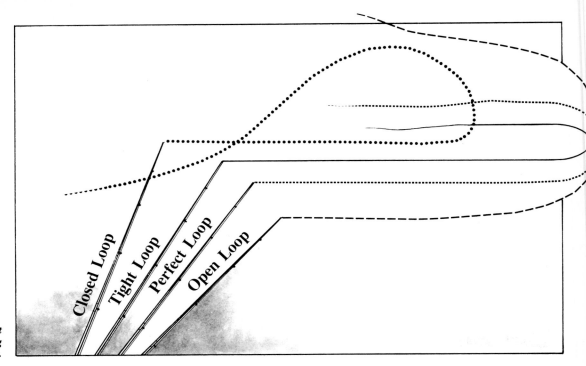

Closed Loop

Tight Loop

Perfect Loop

Open Loop

Loop control is important when adapting your casting to varying conditions.

only success can bring. The greatest challenges will bring the greatest rewards and the angling moments you will cherish forever. Soon the student will become the master.

And, when this happens, we hope you'll take the time to help others you encounter along the same path.

Preparation

Whether you're off to a local pond for bass and panfish or headed for the back country of Alaska or New Zealand, the foundation of any successful trip is thorough preparation.

There is nothing more frustrating than that moment in the field when you realize you have solved the riddle, you know what to do but don't have the tackle or ability to do it. Whether it's forgetting a piece of tackle, an inability to tie knots correctly or not being able to locate a piece of water you want to fish, these are the kinds of things that can absolutely ruin a wonderful trip.

Let's look at some important ways you can buy some "trip insurance."

Travel Agents *Don't let your dreams become nightmares*

For the individual contemplating one of those dream trips, there is no better way to start your preparation than a visit with a travel agent who specializes in fly fishing trips.

Our Advice: The Number One method for finding a good trip and locating a reliable travel agent is through a referral from a trusted friend.

If you don't have such a friend, the next best thing is to look for travel agents who specialize in fly fishing trips. Just like an independent insurance agent, these trip brokers are not tied to any one location or lodge. The good ones recommend the best place for your particular needs. And how do they know about such places? They spend lots of time visiting the destinations they recommend, locating new spots and staying in touch with older ones. A good agent will make sure you don't go to a lodge with a big reputation where the "wine is sweet and the fishing is sour!" Sometimes it happens. Through poor management practices, the fishing at a quality lodge can deteriorate and be a shocking disappointment to the angler who stays there.

These agents can be worth their weight in gold when looking for that special trip of a lifetime. Such a trip is usually expensive, so this is no time to cut corners or gamble. So look around for an experienced agent. Most advertise in the fly fishing

Agents can be worth their weight in gold when looking for that special trip of a lifetime.

magazines and attend the sport shows. Once you find one, don't be afraid to ask for references of people you can contact about the services you can expect. And, when interviewing an agent, remember: the best agents ask the most questions. That's because they're trying to find out what needs you have so they can suggest the right place for you.

Practice
An investment that pays big dividends

Despite the best of intentions, finding the time to practice is a problem we all have. One way to deal with this is to set up your rod and leave it near an entry way after practicing. Then, several times a week, grab the rod when you get home in the evening or in any spare moment and practice 10 to 15 minutes. You'll be surprised how quickly your casting improves and how much fun practicing can be when you eliminate the little things that keep you from it.

Whatever routine you develop, be sure to include time for the basics as well as the new techniques you're working on, especially the ones you think you're most likely to encounter on your next trip. And don't always practice in fair weather. Pick some blustery days to deal with those special problems of casting in the wind and see how much you improve your performance (and your attitude) the next time you encounter those conditions in the field.

As for the practice sessions, most good casters set up drills that will simulate situations they will face on the water. Use your lawn, a park or local schoolyard. Pretend specific features are parts of a river and practice "casting around the clock" with different casts. Some anglers even "wade" their lawn and cast to holding spots!

See the *Advanced Fly Casting* video.

The other area of expertise that should get some practice time is knot tying. Again, practicing what you know to increase speed and efficiency plus working on new things should be part of each session. You can never spend too much time on the knots you use for tying on a fly or adding tippet material. A good fly fisher can literally tie these knots in the dark, something you should try when you think you're getting good at this!

Billy Pate, for instance, keeps his knot-tying skills finely honed by tying the Bimini Twists he'll need for the morning while

bouncing over the flats at 40 mph! Be sure to use lots of different tippet sizes and tie outdoors in cold or windy conditions once in awhile. It will really build your confidence. Also, spend a little time on those knots you might rarely use—a nail or a blood knot—just so you'll be able to tie one in an emergency. How maddening to have your leader break at the line and not be able to connect it again!

Organization
Don't make the most memorable part of your trip what you forgot

Whether it's your tackle, flies, waders, vest or whatever you use, organizing your fly fishing gear will pay you back many times over. Leaving behind the proper piece of equipment will force you to use

Valentine Atkinson

The stuff mid-winter dreams are made of.

the wrong thing in a specific situation and to suffer the consequences.

One of the great things about fly fishing is all the stuff you need. For the gear buff, fly fishing is the ultimate sport. Everything from little doodads for your vest to high-tech wading boots will, over the years, find its way into your hands and closet! But such acquisitions can also be a curse if they aren't organized properly so you can get what you need when you need it.

"I can't take everything I own, but I

don't want to leave something behind that I'll need!" This is Everyman's fly fishing dilemma. Its solution will require careful, thoughtful planning before you head out to fish. So, be sure you work out a system to organize your gear. One that works. Here's where you can use the Formula For Success in another way. Just apply the formula to the fishing that lies ahead and make notes on the appropriate gear you'll need. Then begin the process of organizing the items: the flies, lines, reels, rods, etc. This approach will, of course, only be as effective as your understanding of what your needs will be.

Our Advice: When in doubt, take it.

If you fish streams or rivers, the single most important item for organizing your gear is your vest. If you look at it as a filing cabinet, you'll be amazed at how much more useful it will be. Most anglers take the time before they leave to load their vest with the needs of the day. And, if you are lucky enough to fish someday with a master angler, you will notice they usually go for the vest with lots of pockets. It's not that they always keep them full, but they've learned that even though it makes for tougher walking, a carefully filled vest will reduce your odds of leaving behind an important piece of tackle or box of flies.

One way to lighten that load is to substitute plastic for metal where you can, particularly the fly boxes. It's hard to believe, but it will make a huge difference after a day on the water. Another good trick is to put your extra spools in the back of your vest to counterbalance your load in the front. Your wading in swift currents will be more secure with this arrangement.

Some days, your organizing efforts will be the most important thing you do on your trip, so it's worth the effort to organize your gear for every outing. Besides, most anglers really enjoy sorting through things before a trip. Your imagination will start running wild as you recall past experiences and project yourself into the events so close at hand. And, when you've finished the job, you'll discover there's a lot of satisfaction knowing you're in good shape for the exciting times ahead.

Information

The more you know, the more fun you'll have

Whether you are fishing your favorite piece of local water or one of the storied waters of the fly fishing world, it's helpful to collect and evaluate as much information about the waters you fish as you can find. Such data, which can come from many sources, will be invaluable in applying the Formula for Success to your fishing. It is also one of the things about fly fishing that makes it so interesting.

Many anglers enjoy keeping some sort of a fishing journal. Whether you buy one or make it up yourself, a systematic record of your fishing experiences will be very helpful in future outings. The more detailed, the more useful. What such records will reveal in time are certain patterns that tell you about fish location and feeding habits plus the fly patterns and presentation methods that work.

For example, trout anglers record insect hatches they encounter on the stream and, learning from this experience, can plan successful future outings around these predictable hatching cycles. Some anglers have total recall about their fishing. Most don't. So the active fly fisher will make a careful review of fishing journals an important part of the trip preparation. Maintaining the journal is just as essential.

Good sources of information about famous waters are the fly fishing books, magazines and videos. Part of the fun of planning a big trip is researching a specific location. You can pick up all sorts of ideas about tackle, presentation techniques and places to fish that can prepare you to fish new water. Some fly fishers will photocopy or clip the best articles and file them away with their fishing journal for future reference should they fish these waters again.

While print sources are a very important part of preparing for any trip, they are limited in what they can do. Their main purpose is to create enthusiasm for fishing in a specific location and to prepare you for what you'll find there. But, with the recent video revolution, anglers now have a tremendous resource that can make their days on the water very comfortable and productive. For example, a video that actually shows you a famous piece of water you'll fish, like the flats in Florida or the Henry's Fork in Idaho, will help you feel right at home when you get there. You'll know the kinds of water you're going to fish, the conditions you're likely to face and can prepare yourself for success.

But the most important advantage of videos over print is they show exactly what you need to do in the situations and

With the recent video revolution, anglers now have a tremendous resource.

conditions you encounter. If, for example, you are going to fish a still water location for trout, seeing the actual techniques you'll use and taking time to practice before you leave on the trip will have you taking fish right away. None of this on-the-job training!

This will be especially true when it comes to something totally different from any fly fishing you've ever done, like tarpon fishing, Some anglers literally experience "culture shock" when they fish the flats and encounter their first tarpon. But, with some time spent viewing videos on tarpon fishing and working on presentation techniques, you can feel very comfortable your first day on the flats. There's simply nothing you can read that will help you understand what you need to do with your first tarpon.

As anglers discover the many advantages of fly fishing videos, we have seen a trend develop in recent years: fly fishing video libraries. Many anglers enjoy reading about the sport and have impressive collections of fly fishing books that are part of an old and rich literary tradition. But

Maps

*A*nother way to supplement your reading about a fishing location is to acquire maps of the area and study them. There are two sources that can help: fly shop owners and the U.S. Department of the Interior.

More and more tackle dealers have produced maps they are happy to send you. Although such maps will sometimes lack detail, the best ones give a very clear picture of that water and can even include likely holding places for fish. Often, these maps will include information about popular fly patterns you may want to tie or buy before you arrive. These maps are fine for getting you to the most popular spots with the right flies and a good idea of the tackle you'll need.

But, for the more adventurous angler who craves isolation and the chance to explore new water, the topo maps prepared by the U.S. Department of the Interior are essential. Available from tackle shops and the U.S. Forest Service, these detailed maps are perfect for those times

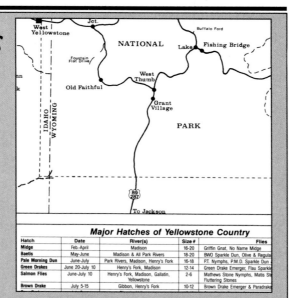

Major Hatches of Yellowstone Country				
Hatch	Date	River(s)	Size #	Flies
Midge	Feb-April	Madison	16-20	Griffin Gnat, No Name Midge
Baetis	May-June	Madison & All Park Rivers	18-20	BWO Sparkle Dun, Olive & Regular
Pale Morning Dun	June-July	Park Rivers, Madison, Henry's Fork	16-18	P.T. Nymphs, P.M.D. Sparkle Dun
Green Drakes	June 20-July 10	Henry's Fork, Madison	12-14	Green Drake Emerger, Flau Sparkle
Salmon Flies	June-July 10	Henry's Fork, Madison, Gallatin, Yellowstone	2-6	Mathews Stone Nymphs, Matis St Fluttering Stones
Brown Drake	July 5-15	Gibbon, Henry's Fork	10-12	Brown Drake Emerger & Paradrake

Map courtesy of Craig and Jackie Matheus of Blue Ribbon Flies, West Yellowstone, Montana.

you want to fish remote locations, like alpine lakes or anywhere in the Back Country. And, don't overlook the value of topo maps on your Home Waters. A careful scanning might reveal a new access road or a route that requires a hike to a stretch other anglers have overlooked and may lead to some exceptional fishing.

Our Advice: many of the famous waters you want to fish are awfully big, so study your maps carefully before you arrive if you plan to tackle them on your own. Maps found in books and magazine articles will help you identify the popular access points and other good places to start. But getting your hands on tackle shop maps or topos can provide important additional details that will complete your preparation. It can be awfully frustrating and disappointing to travel great distances and take on one of the big rivers like Montana's Yellowstone or Madison without some help before hand.

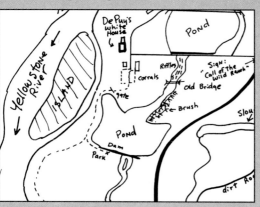

Map courtesy of George Anderson of the Yellowstone Angler, Livingston, Montana.

many of today's high-tech fly fishers are sticking videos on their shelves, too, and viewing them repeatedly as they develop their angling skills. They've discovered that the best tapes are loaded with information that they need to see many times over to fully understand as they move down the path to fly fishing mastery. In this way, videos are an excellent value compared to books that are often read only once.

But a word of caution: all videos are not created equal. Since the first videos came out in 1982, over 75 titles are now available and, as you might imagine, the quality and prices vary. You'll see everything from tapes that are not much more than home movies to full scale movie productions. While production may not be everything, content certainly is the most important quality in a video. You'll get the best value from a well-organized, fast-moving tape that's loaded with information and instruction you can use over and over. In the same way a good instructional book must be re-read to learn the lessons it has to teach, so too are the best videos full of concepts and techniques you'll need to see repeatedly in order to master them.

The best way to choose a video is to preview the tape. This "look before you leap" strategy is the best approach to building a video library because you'll soon know which tapes best suit your needs. Renting tapes from your local tackle dealer or favorite cataloger will save you a lot of money that might be wasted on poor tapes. It will also reveal an exciting, powerful

source of instruction and entertainment that will help you improve your fly fishing skills. Today's videos cover just about everything from the basic skills to the most advanced presentation techniques all filmed in the most exciting fly fishing locations in the world.

One other great source of information are area fly fishers. A little bit of local knowledge offered by tackle dealers and guides can be priceless. The fellows in the shop usually have an excellent overview of the fishing in their area and the best ones are happy to share it with you. With a steady stream of guides and other anglers pouring through the shop each day, the shopkeepers can give lots of good advice on location, flies and presentation techniques. But, if they run a guide service, don't expect them to give away everything in great detail. That's the guide's job. And you will find it's a good investment to hire a guide for a few days and learn more about new water. The virtues of a good guide have been extolled since the first ghilly and, considering the time these men and women give to obtain this information, it comes very cheap.

These are some of the basic sources of information that you can apply to the Formula for Success and increase your angling pleasure. There are others. But, whatever you choose to explore, collect this information in a systematic way and use it in the field. The longer you fish, the more important such information will become to you.

A permit on a fly... an angling treasure.

Brian O'Keefe

Organizations

Scientific Anglers is concerned about the future of our environment, especially our aquatic resources. Many of us on the SA team are active members of conservation organizations and, as a company, we have made a financial commitment to these groups.

But, with so many organizations working toward common goals, it's difficult to decide which ones to support. The primary criteria we use to determine our level of commitment is the organization's ability to make a positive impact on the resource.

Based on our knowledge and experience, we support the following organizations:

Trout Unlimited
Fly Fishing Federation
Florida Keys Fishing Guides Association
SEACOPS
Gulf Coast Conservation Association
Atlantic Salmon Federation
Camp Fish
American Museum of Fly Fishing
Catskill Fly Fishing Center
International Gamefish Association
National Freshwater Fishing Hall of Fame
Sport Fishing Institute
American Fishing Tackle Manufacturers
    Association
North American Fly Tackle Trade
    Association

The Logic of a Scientist, the Emotions of a Madman

A delicate balancing act

Most people come to fly fishing and stay with it a lifetime because they are attracted to the sport, then fall in love with it. It becomes one of the great passions in their life. There is so much to excite us: catching a fish on a fly we tied, finding a secret spot on our favorite river, taking a memorable trip with a close friend, landing a great fish—such things bring us the joys we find in the angling life. And the great beauty of it all is it can be as simple or complex as we choose.

But, looking back, most of these rewards come from careful evaluation of the things we must do to be successful anglers, then doing these things well. They are really the kinds of things we've considered in this chapter, the things that lead to angling success in the broadest terms. And, if we are to enjoy the rich and varied successes fly fishing can provide, we must keep the science behind the art close at all times.

So often and so easily, we find ourselves caught up completely in the excitement of the moment and lose sight of the important principles that will bring us success. It's the first day of your fishing trip and the fish begin to feed wildly. You starting casting the first fly that jumps out of your box, only to be frustrated by constant rejection. Others around you are catching fish, but not you. At such times, you will need to bring all you've learned to the moment—all the parts of the Formula for Success—and apply them to the situation at hand.

Or, you are fishing a piece of water that you are certain holds some good fish that are feeding deep. Time and again, you present the right fly at the right level and you do it correctly. You are certain. But there are no strikes. Others around you are using another strategy and they are taking fish. Small ones but lots of them. You question everything about the Formula for Success and your ability to apply it. At such moments, you will need all the mental toughness you've got to stick with this approach if you want to take the bigger fish you pursue. Only then will you solve the riddle and find the joys you seek.

Just being aware of this side of your angling experiences is an important part of your preparation to go into the field. The

The Sky is Falling

by Howard West

*L*ike everyone who fishes regularly, I've got my spots. My favorite stretch of water is on a small stream on my way home from our St. Paul office. It's actually near a popular parking spot where anglers begin their hikes through the woods, upstream and down, to the classic pools that draw so many fly fishers to this fertile, freestone stream.

But I'm very pleased my spot gets passed by. It's only 200 feet of narrow stream, but the towering hardwoods and the peaceful sounds of the water always wash away the stress and the battles lost at the office. Usually, I just ease into the quiet currents near the bank about 30 feet below the tailout, then work my way upstream— slow and easy so I don't push a bow wave— scanning the water for rising fish. The best fish always seem to be in a waist-deep trough that runs along the far bank lined with heavy brush just beneath the hardwoods. Sometimes, if no one else has beat me here, I can even find a few nice fish in shallows no more than a foot deep near this bank.

Many years ago, when I was more driven to catch lots of trout than to ponder the "why's" behind my successes and failures, I slipped out of the office early after asking my secretary to tell any callers that I would be in the lab for the rest of the day. I hiked to "my" spot just as a few of the last remaining sulphur mayflies fluttered to the overhanging trees. Even though the hatch was just about over for the year, I tied on a #16 brownish-colored nymph with split shot and began casting upstream into the deeper slot along the far bank. My first pitch missed the slot by a good six feet— ah, the joys of casting lead—and landed in the shallows.

While laughing off this pitiful excuse for a cast and watching my nymph sink like a pint-sized anvil, a nice brown suddenly darted out of the deeper water and sucked in my nymph before it hit bottom! With reflexes usually far keener and sharper than *(continued on page 58)*

The Sky is Falling, cont.

my mind, I set the hook quick as a cat and popped the 6X tippet before the merest thought could enter my mind. After a hurried look around to make sure there were no spectators to what was becoming quite an exhibition, I tied on another nymph and shot. My next cast was perfect. Right in the slot. I watched the nymph hit the water and, before it had time to sink three inches, I saw the leader slice upstream. Cleverly, I overcompensated slightly and did absolutely nothing!

I was totally stunned. Something was wrong. BIG wrong. Sure, this was one of my "killer" fly patterns, but fish were hitting it before it even sank, practically on top. Other casts brought swirls and flashes but no hook-ups. Then, unaccustomed as I was to solving angling riddles, a glimmer of light seeped slowly into my brain: the fish were obviously attracted to the "plop" of my nymph and shot. Were they feeding on something falling from above, not emerging from below?

Feeling more like a garden variety Isaac Newton than the next Isaac Walton, I tested my new theory with new fly patterns. It was breezy, so I tried ants. Then beetles of various sizes and colors. They could be blown off the trees and brush along the bank, right? I got a few "looks" from the trout, but not one legitimate nose-poke. So much for this theory!

By now, I had invested over two hours trying to solve this intriguing riddle and hadn't laid a glove on 'em. Not even one lousy dink so I could pump his stomach for more information! While not a personal record, or anything, this solid skunking was starting to go beyond disappointment. We were talking runaway, freight train self-doubt, now. Then, thoughts of the beer chilling in the cooler not 200 yards away in the car broke my concentration as I reviewed possible solutions. And, when I remembered the fresh-baked chocolate chip cookies on the front seat, I almost cracked and ran.

But I was too stubborn to give up.

I played "just one more fly" for another hour, suffering the curse of the angler who carries every fly he owns. As pattern after pattern failed, I grubbed frantically through decades worth of dry flies till my eye caught something odd at the bottom of my fly box. It was a fat, 3X long green deer hair worm. Eaaaah! Um. Why not, I

thought. First cast—at least, the first good one—brought the swift, certain rise I had longed for all these hours. "Eureka!" (Was it Newton or Diogenes who said that?) Ten fat Brownies later—all respectfully released, of course—and I had "wormed out" the run and had become the subject of stares from passing anglers. Probably was my ear-to-ear grin. I had solved the riddle they were yet to face.

That night, back in the tying room, I went at it like a man possessed. Green worms in every shade imaginable in sizes 4 to 14 (even some two-tone jobs, 12 segments to the inch!). My mission was clear: return to the "spot" tomorrow and clean house. From the Get-Go, this time.

And, no surprise, I did. I returned to the same water and, doubtlessly, fooled many of the same fish. I was in complete control from beginning to end. A master at the top of his game. It was no longer a question whether I would solve The Riddle. It was really a matter of keeping score. But after taking several nice fish, I stopped. Something was wrong. My grin was fading fast—though the gawkers still gawked as I landed another fish—and I found myself not caring if I landed another "worm eater." The Thrill was definitely gone.

From that day of triumph turned stale, I looked at—no thought about—fly fishing differently. A dramatic shift had taken place. The greatest satisfaction I receive from fly fishing then and now, some 10 years later, comes from Solving the Riddles. Don't get me wrong. I still love to catch fish and it still takes quite a few to satisfy my appetite. But my Super Highs come from cracking the code, the tougher the better!

And, I get just as excited fooling a solid 11-inch brown trout minutes from downtown St. Paul as I do when I figure out the right size, color shade, shape, life cycle stage and number of abdomen segments on the mayfly of the hour being devoured by monster bank-feeders on the Henry's Fork.

It's all so simple. It's the challenge that hooks the deepest. And there's no catch-and-release!

The greatest satisfaction I receive from fly fishing then and now, some 10 years later, comes from Solving the Riddles.

passions that keep you involved with fly fishing will always be there (Let's hope we can always get so excited about fishing that we need to gather our wits!). But the analytical, scientific approach to these experiences needs to be part of it, too. Without the composure to apply your powers of analysis and reason to an angling problem, you will experience moments no less frustrating than the angler who cannot cast far enough or has not brought the equipment necessary to reach feeding fish. You will be equally limited. To be sure, it is often a delicate balance but one the successful angler can maintain.

We hope all this information about the Formula for Success has helped you to learn many new things that will speed you down the road to fly fishing mastery and to the triumphs you will surely enjoy along the way. The seemingly endless variety of new concepts and skills is one of the things that makes fly fishing a lifetime adventure. The excitement and satisfaction of knowing the "Why's" of the experiences you have, the thrill of solving the riddle of the most challenging angling situations, is the ultimate angling High. And, maybe best of all, there always seems to be one more bend at the end of the river!

In the next chapter, "Solving the Riddle," you'll see how the Formula for Success and the principles we've discussed can be applied to angling problems in the field. We'll let some master anglers tell you about some challenging angling situations they encountered and how they used the presentation part of the Formula to solve the problem.

A Scientific Anglers History:

From silk lines to microballoons

*B*efore modern equipment was developed, even the most talented fly fishers who practiced long and hard could only achieve modest results. If you ever get a chance to see the early tackle in a museum or personal collection, you'll be amazed at what they used in the Good Old Days. (Some modern anglers feel the old equipment is the best argument that fish were easier to take in the early days!) Large, heavy rods and reels. And silk lines that had to be dried and treated every night to get a few hours of poor floatation the next day. In those days, a balanced fly fishing system wasn't an option. You bought the components where you could find them, learned to use what you had and made the best of it.

If you talked to any fly fisher of that era, they would have told you the single greatest need they had was for a fly line that would float high and be convenient to use. So, when a couple of serious fly fishers from Midland, Michigan, Clare Harris and Leon Martuch, got together from time to time, that's the problem they talked about solving. They knew first hand what it was like to deal with those old lines and they also had the scientific, creative skills to do something about the matter. So, in 1945, they started a company called Scientific Anglers and first sold two new products they had developed, a silicone-based fly floatant and magnesium rod tubes.

While these products kept the company going, these two inventive men worked in their kitchen on the fly line of their dreams. By the 1940's and 50's, fly line manufacturers had begun to experiment with some new materials like nylon but couldn't solve

Scientific Anglers' founder, Leon Martuch, working in his kitchen on the early prototypes of the Air Cel®, the first modern floating fly line.

The fly fishers of the 90's have equipment that is the result of all that science has to offer.

Scientific Anglers manufacturing plant in Midland, Michigan.

the riddle. While Clare and Leon didn't have fancy labs and assistants, they did have their own ideas about what to do with that nylon. Working on their kitchen stove to coat a braided nylon line with polyvinylchloride, they developed a revolutionary product: a tapered, plastic-coated line that didn't need a dressing to float. The Air Cel line, introduced in 1952, was the first of its kind and became the standard for all modern fly lines.

The revolution, however, had just begun and, in the years that followed, the original scientific anglers perfected their floating fly line technology and developed new lines for a growing market. They moved out of their kitchen into a brand new plant where they cooked up sinking lines that sank at precise rates, specialty tapers to handle the presentation needs of bass and saltwater anglers, sinking tip and shooting head lines that greatly increased the effective range of all fly fishers. The sport of fly fishing was coming into its own during the 60's and the new generation of modern fly lines increased the effectiveness and angling pleasure of all fly fishers who explored the potential of the sport.

SA addressed the other important need that fly fishers had—tackle components that didn't work well together—and introduced

a concept that was almost as revolutionary as the floating line—the Balanced System. By adding rods and reels to its product line, Scientific Anglers started manufacturing and selling the first balanced fly fishing systems, components that were designed to work together.

During this expansion period, SA purchased the "microballoons" used in the coating of floating lines from the 3M company. In time, this relationship flourished and, at the direction of company executive, Lew Jewett, 3M purchased Scientific Anglers in 1973, a marriage of fly fishing expertise and modern research technology that has produced the most innovative fly fishing concepts and products on the market today.

Through the years, the company grew and new people joined the SA team, but they continued to follow the lead of the company founders. They listened to the needs of the customer and developed new products to meet those needs. Other Air Cel® floating lines and the Wet Cel® sinking lines and Wet Tip® floating/sinking lines were added. Lines that floated higher, sank faster and cast easier joined their respective family of lines and were eagerly spooled on the reels of anglers who pursued new species all over the world.

Today, the lines are still developed and manufactured in our plant in Midland where the grouse still drum in the woods. And the folks that work there, like our founders, are fly fishermen and quick to take the latest prototype lines hot off the machine to the casting pool just outside the front door. But that's about the only thing that hasn't changed. The Midland plant, which now manufactures more fly lines than any plant in the world, produces the prototype lines for testing and all the lines that end up on our customers' reels. But they certainly don't work alone.

The Scientific Anglers lab, sales and customer service people are all located in the 425-acre 3M Center in St. Paul, Minnesota, which they share with over 13,000 other talented employees. Their job is to keep listening to the customer and finding better ways to serve their needs. Whether it's systems of fly lines, reels or information all designed to improve the angling success and pleasure of fly fishers worldwide, the Scientific Anglers staff knows about fly fishing. You're just as likely to find these people on the flats of Belize or the rushing

rivers of British Columbia as the local trout streams and bass lakes of Minnesota or Michigan. The needs of today's fly fishers may be more varied, but like Clare and Leon, the SA staff knows first hand what fly fishers want wherever they enjoy their sport.

Because of people on the Scientific Anglers teams that have run the company since the 1940's and developed the line of innovative products, the fly fishers of the 90's have equipment that is the result of all that science has to offer. Space-age materials, designs developed in modern research facilities and supported by thousands of hours of field testing and manufacturing standards that produce components that work together. Today's equipment and information about how to use it has dramatically narrowed the gap between the skills of an enthusiastic amateur angler and the dedicated professional. And, with these innovations have come the opportunity for the highest angling pleasures and success of any generation of fly fishers.

Leon with a magnesium fly rod case, an early Scientific Anglers product that helped finance the first generation of modern fly lines.

Solving the Riddle

Valentine Atkinson

*A*fter our discussion of those key principles in the "Foundations of Fly Fishing" chapter, here's where we show you the presentation part of the Formula for Success in action.

We asked a dozen Master Anglers to describe how they solved a presentation problem they encountered fishing for trout, steelhead, bass, bonefish and tarpon. As we've said, presentation is really the heart of fly fishing mastery and the one part of the Formula that can improve your angling success faster than anything else.

In the following articles, you'll recognize the names of many of these Master Anglers. They are widely published and, in some instances, have appeared in their own instructional videos. Others, may not be so familiar—that is, unless you've been fortunate to have joined them on one of their guided fishing trips.

But all these anglers have three things in common: they spend a large amount of time fly fishing for various species of fish on many different waters and they are always developing new ways to improve their angling success.

Third, and maybe most important, these hard-core fly fishers all have a strong commitment to using the Formula for Success to handle any angling situation they face. They have confidence in it because it's worked for them through the years handling problems more varied and challenging than most of us could come across in three lifetimes.

We think these personal experiences will help you understand the principles of presentation we discussed in the "Foundations of Fly Fishing" chapter and show you some ways they can be applied to your own experiences.

The Science Behind the Art

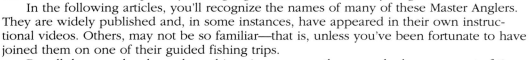

Sometimes you'll have to be able to cast a line long to catch steelhead.

A Hot Time on the Tarpon Flats

by George Anderson

PROFILE: *Proprietor of the Yellowstone Angler, a well-known fly fishing shop in Livingston, Montana, George is a former fly fishing guide. He has fished throughout the West and Northwest (including Alaska) and has also gained vast saltwater experience—notably in Florida and Central America. His articles on fishing and hunting have been published in numerous magazines. An expert fly tyer, he has developed two nymph patterns that are extremely popular patterns on Western streams—the Peeking Caddis and George's Brown Stone.*

---

*I*t was late spring in Key West. Jim Smith and I were there to fish tarpon and I was anxious to try a new clear, braided monofilament core fly line Scientific Anglers had just developed.

We were out on the beautiful ocean side flats near Woman Key and there were plenty of tarpon cruising over these white sand, hard coral flats. But, with a high sun, the fish hugged the bottom in six to seven feet of water, moving fast, and were unusually tough to take.

I had started with a floating line, but it just didn't allow the fly to get down quickly enough to interest the fast-moving fish. After I had blown a couple of easy shots at fish, Jim tried his blue intermediate sinking line. A string of four fish appeared, but they never saw Jim's fly as the cast fell short. When the next group of perhaps twenty fish appeared, Jim made a perfect cast and the fly appeared to be lined up right on the lead fish. But the fish didn't take! Then, when Jim started to strip the fly, the whole school simply blew up and headed for deeper water. We just stared at each other and shook our heads.

It looked like just a long, hot day on the flats if we didn't do something different.

George Anderson and Key West companion.

63

As the sun burned down on us, I wondered if the bright day with exceptionally clear water conditions weren't at the heart of our problem. Maybe this was the time to try the new sinking Tarpon Taper line. In a matter of moments, I had peeled the floating line off my reel and replaced it with the new nearly-clear line.

As soon as I started stripping the new line off the reel onto the deck, I could see one big advantage over the standard lines: with its stiffness, the Tarpon Taper had far less tendency to tangle. And, when I cast it, the slick finish let the line shoot through the guides like a bullet. Wet or dry, it cast better than any saltwater line I'd ever used.

I passed the rod over to Jim and asked him to try the new line. Just as he began to cast, our guide spotted a huge school of tarpon, over 75 fish, headed our way. Jim quickly double-hauled, making a perfect cast that put the fly dead in front of the fast-moving school. After pausing to let the fly sink, he began his retrieve. The lead fish in the school was already past the fly now, but Jim continued to strip. Suddenly, a tarpon in the middle of the school flashed, turning and lunging at the fly. Jim smacked him hard. The fish hit the air for two head-shaking jumps before throwing the hook. Wow! That was more like it!

Jim and I were laughing now. We were disappointed to lose a good fish but encouraged that we had taken a fish out of the middle of a school under such difficult conditions. For the rest of the day, we switched off, using my rod. That afternoon, we jumped three more tarpon, landing one over 80 pounds. It was a great day. We had lots of fun and learned a valuable lesson: the clear-coated sinking Tarpon Taper lines were nearly invisible in the water and this made them far less likely to spook fish than the standard lines we had used for years.

The hot tropical mid-day sun makes fish spooky but it also softens standard fly lines, especially when they are stripped out on the casting deck or bottom of the boat. They seem to turn almost rubbery and won't shoot well through the guides. But, with the new lines, we didn't have that problem at all. In fact, they made casting a pleasure even in the hottest conditions we faced on the trip. The line has also practically eliminated the tangles and bird's nests I used to get in my shooting line while casting or clearing line onto the reel. Since using the Tarpon Taper, I'm losing less fish to break-offs from a wad of tangled line that gets caught in my guides and spending more time fishing than straightening out line.

Scientific Anglers now makes these braided monofilament core lines in both sinking and floating versions. With performance characteristics superior to standard lines in tropical climates, these new lines have fast become the favorites of all saltwater anglers and a standard part of my fly fishing system.

The "moment of truth" for guide Craig Brewer.

Howard West

Getting a Line on Snails

by Gary Borger

✑ PROFILE: *One of the country's most popular fly fishing columnists and magazine writers, Gary has also published two of the best-selling books on fly fishing—* Naturals *and* Nymphing: A Basic Book. *In addition, Gary is one of video's most prolific presenters, having completed three instructional videos for Scientific Anglers as well as eight other videos for his own company. He is presently at work on a new book about tying and fishing his own fly patterns and three new videos.*

*M*uch fly fishing romance has been attached to mayflies, sedges, midges, stoneflies, damselflies and even sculpins. But snails, somehow, are not creatures that capture the imagination of fly fishers. As "escargot," they are a gustatory marvel. But to fish with one? The thought seems ludicrous. But trout in lakes do eat snails and eat them in vast quantities. And, in the eating, they create for the fly fisher some very specific presentation problems that can be neatly solved by judicious line selection.

I first experienced significant fishing success with snail patterns late one June as Bob Pelzl and I fished the lakes of Vermejo Park Ranch in New Mexico. It had been a so-so day. A fish here, a fish there. But no consistency. So we began experimenting. Bob tied on a Peacock Nymph and cast it out. As he stood counting down his Wet Cel II sinking line, a fish grabbed the fly so violently that the tippet broke! Bob told me what happened, then tied on another fly and cast out into the same area. This time, he paid close attention as the fly sunk and, when another fish hit his imitation, Bob was ready. Just as I arrived, Bob lifted the fish from the water. We stared at one another as we heard the snail shells in its stomach grind like a handful of gravel! That incident began a decade of investigation for us into the life habits of snails and how trout feed on them.

One problem we encountered early on was how to most effectively fish a snail pattern. We were in a bit of a quandary because snails mostly live in dense beds of aquatic weeds and because they move so

slowly. True. You will find them on near-shore rocks and slowly creeping about on sunken logs. But take a look in the aquatic plants and you'll realize that this is the true home of the snail. In some lakes, snail populations run in the millions. Such an abundant food source is not ignored by trout which actually root around in sunken weed beds searching for snails.

To get our fly patterns down to the sunken weed beds where most of the snails are found and to keep the fly in the fish's feeding zone, we found the most effective choice was a full sinking line.

In water over 10 feet deep, we use a Wet Cel II because it sinks fast enough to probe deeper waters, but is not so fast that the angler can't control the fly's depth by the rate of retrieve. A long, fast strip planes the fly up. A slow retrieve allows the line to continue to sink. When fishing the sunken snail pattern with this line, we count the line down until it reaches the proper depth. We give it one long, fast strip, then wait 10 to 15 seconds. The process is repeated until the entire line has been retrieved. This retrieving method pulls the line up a bit, then lets it sink a bit, keeping the line just above the weeds and giving the snail pattern a rising-sinking action that is deadly.

But, mostly, when fishing a sunken snail imitation, we use an intermediate sinking line because it solves a variety of sticky snail fishing problems. Most often, sunken snail imitations are fished in relatively shallow water (less than eight feet deep) and other sinking lines simply sink too fast. The very slow sink rate of the intermediate line allows the alternating strip-rest-strip retrieve to keep the line out of the plants.

The biggest advantage of the intermediate line, however, is when the wind comes up and creates waves. A wave is not just a surface phenomenon. It is a wheel of water, rolling through the lake with only one-eighth of its height sticking above the surface. As it rolls through the near-shore weed beds, the wave sweeps the snails from the plants and carries them to open water. So, when the wind is up, that's where you find trout, cruising about eagerly and feeding on the hapless mollusks. A snail imitation fished in the open water above a weed bed during these windy periods will often produce fish in quantities that will astound even the veteran fly fisher.

But there are some problems fishing in

Gary Borger

these conditions that the intermediate lines can solve most effectively.

While the high, sometimes gale-force winds stir the pot that cooks up such a tasty feast for the trout, such winds can also make casting an absolute nightmare. But Bob and I discovered that a double-haul cast for extra line speed combined with the narrow diameter of the intermediate sinking line enables us to cast in high winds with astonishing ease. It gave us the control we needed to make accurate casts and eliminated the fatigue of fighting the wind all day. Once on the water, the intermediate line sinks through the turbulent surface water and, thus, is not blown around by the wind like a floating line. And, as it sinks, it will stay below the surface and keeps our fly where we want it despite the upswelling surges of the waves.

Once the wind dies down, snails are often found floating in the surface film and, no surprise, the trout are right there, sucking them from the film and leaving a strong rise form reminiscent of trout feeding on caddis pupae. Such activity can confound the fly fisher unless a few moments are spent searching for the food item. Once we have determined that trout are feeding on floating snails, we often rig up an intermediate line and treat it with fly floatant. This gives us all the advantages of a floating line—sitting low in the surface film—while still enabling us to make long, effortless casts into a breeze.

The final advantage of an intermediate line and its thin diameter comes into play when fighting fish. One attractive feature of fishing for trout in lakes is their size which is much greater on the average than their cousins in the streams and rivers. When playing these larger fish, you'll find they often make long, powerful runs, dragging a great deal of line from your reel before surrendering to the net. The drag from all that line being towed about in the water by the panic-stricken trout creates a great strain on the tippet. The thin diameter of the intermediate sinking line, however, will lessen this drag by about one-half over a floating line of the same weight.

Needless to say, I am convinced intermediate sinking lines are an essential item for the tackle bag of the stillwater fly fisher. And not just because of their usefulness in fishing snail patterns. On a recent trip to South Africa, the trout streams and lakes I fished were beset by strong winds and rains. But I went first to my intermediate sinking line and captured the biggest fish of the trip fishing a minnow imitation over a sunken weed bed. During the course of my fishing season, I will use the intermediate line for fishing fly patterns of other creatures such as mayfly, damselfly and dragonfly nymphs, caddis and midge pupa, backswimmers and waterboatmen, scuds and leeches.

As you can see, the intermediate sinking line is an important part of the fly line system for the stillwater angler. Its many advantages—particularly over a floating line—will make your fishing more enjoyable and productive whether you're getting a line on snails or any of the other abundant food sources you'll find in lakes.

Sometimes you need to put a long, careful sneak on a fish before you cast.

Valentine Atkinson

Alligator Rises

by Bob Clay

PROFILE: *Bob learned about fly fishing from well-known angler, Harold Honer, and developed his angling skills on the famous Bow River in Alberta, Canada. But, once he discovered steelheading in the early 70's, that was it for Bob! He moved to the Kispiox Valley in 1977 where he started a family and the Water Ouzel Fly Fishing Guide Service. Bob has been fishing this area and showing clients the wonderful steelhead fishing since 1977.*

*L*ike most steelhead fly fishers, I started out using subsurface methods to take these fish in heavy currents and, later, when I started guiding, that's how my clients fished. But, over the past few years, things have changed. More and more of my clients want to fish for these powerful giants on top and, once they've experienced the thrill of taking steelhead this way, it's hard to turn them! I know just how they feel. I've really enjoyed discovering new ways for my clients to take steelhead on the surface and I find myself using these methods every chance I get.

Let me tell you about the techniques I use.

Not so long ago, anglers felt the only time to take steelhead on top was during the heat of summer when the water temperature is up and the fish's reflexes are razor sharp. And, when summer turned to fall and the water temperature dropped, everyone felt it was time to go deep with the wet fly. But, now, we have discovered you can take these steelhead on the surface at all water temperatures, including the fall season.

The key to success is locating these fish and using the right presentation methods.

In the fall months, steelhead really slow down. A fly travelling quickly will be past him before he can react to it. So, to be successful, you've got to fish slower water which now holds higher levels of oxygen and is more comfortable for the steelhead. (This is usually water that held no fish in summer because the water temperature was too high.) In this type of water, the fish simply have more time to react to our flies.

There are two types of slower water: one you can see, the other you can't.

The water easiest to locate is at the sides of the main current. Steelhead will move close to shore in this slow, shallow water because the sun is lower on the horizon and its rays won't directly penetrate the water (the water will actually look darker now than earlier in the season). The low light levels also make the steelhead feel safe and confident in these locations. The other type of water you need to find is quicker on top and slower on the bottom. To find it, look for structure. Big rocks and ledges on the river's edge are good indicators.

Once you've found water most likely to hold fish and slow enough so they can react in time to take your fly, you'll need to keep several things in mind when choosing the best ways to present your fly.

The main principle is **slow**. The longer the fish can look at your fly, the better your chances of getting them to come up for it. Your fly will also have to have the right **motion** to give it a lifelike appearance. Whether steelhead strike out of territorial aggression or a pre-migrant feeding imprint, this motion will trigger the rise. And the way to get the proper motion is by controlled drag or causing the fly to move just slightly faster than the current. The way to get that control is proper mending, either upstream to slow down the fly or downstream to speed it up.

Traditionally, the best type of floating line for mending was the double taper. It's large belly diameter made it easy to control but also hard to cast any distance. The weight forward, on the other hand, was great for distance but its thin running line made it harder to mend. There's a new line out, now, made by Scientific Anglers called the Steelhead Taper. It mends like a double taper and casts like a weight forward. They've designed the line with a longer front taper, belly section and rear taper to combine the best of both worlds.

Now, let's take a look at how to put this all together.

First, we'll move into the river about ankle deep and cover the slower inside water that's easy to see. I like to use about 30 to 40 feet of line out of the rod (this gives me a total of 45 to 55 feet from my

Bob Clay and an "alligator-rising" steelhead.

Howard West

A sleek Babine hen.

hand to the fly), quartering it downstream and mending line to keep the fly moving just slightly faster than the current. Keep this distance and fly speed constant as you work downstream, one giant step after every cast. Once the fly is directly below you, extend the rod so the fly can travel a little farther. And watch out! Even though you can get a strike anywhere, many rises come at the end of the drift when fish that have followed the fly finally catch up with it.

One of the best things about fishing steelhead on top is the rise. Like the speed of the water and your fly, the rise is also very slow and deliberate. Very often you'll get what I call the "Alligator Rise." You see the top of the fish's head out of the water as it moves to your fly with its jaws opening, then snapping down on your fly! Now is the time to be very slow yourself. Once the fly disappears, raise your rod tip slowly, feeling the weight of the fish, then set the hook. If somehow you don't hook up, wait a minute. Then make the same cast again.

If you can't bring the fish back up in two or three more casts, there are several things you can try. Personally, I like to start with a #4 moose hair bomber, a fly with a highly visible forward wing, as a searching pattern. If I get refusals, I move down in size to a #6 or #8. If I still have no luck, I change the silhouette by using a hackled bivisible. As a last resort, I'll try a slimly dressed wet fly riffle hitched. I can't tell you

how many times this fly has saved the day. If, after trying all these patterns, you still can't move the fish, mark his location and try him again after you've fished out the run.

On your next pass over this water, move out further (say, up to your knees). You'll be casting to water that's a little faster on the surface and slower near the bottom where rocks and ledges are breaking the current. Here's where you really need to work at controlling the fly speed. To do this, cast a longer line at a steeper downstream angle and let the fly wake slowly in a narrow arc, mending if necessary. For this presentation method, I almost always use Lani Waller's fly, the Waller Waker. It really shines! Because this fly planes well and disturbs the water, the steelhead notice it and will come up from their slow water lie through the deeper, faster water to take it.

It has taken many years to solve the riddle of taking steelhead on top in the fall, but these methods have consistently produced for me and my clients who fish these great waters in British Columbia. I hope you'll try these techniques on steelhead sometime. If you do, I promise you some of your greatest angling thrills when you take these magnificent fish on top.

(By the way: if you hook the first steelhead that makes one of those "alligator rises" to your fly, give yourself a pat on the back!)

An Ace in the Hole

by Jim Butler

PROFILE: *Jim grew up on New York's Long Island in the heart of suburban America and, after a brief encounter with the book publishing business, found his way to Maine where he lives with his wife and is Managing Editor of Fly Rod & Reel magazine. ("Thanks to Nick Lyons' prodding," says Jim.) Jim spends most of his days thinking, writing and talking about fly fishing, activities most readers would envy. The rest of the time, he gets in as much fly fishing as possible and enjoys solving angling problems on waters from Maine to Labrador (Alaska is next on the list).*

*F*ly fishing in the Caribbean. Ah, at last! My first trip to the flats of Belize was preceded with great anticipation and lots of reading. Books and articles by Joe Brooks, Lefty Kreh and others alerted me to a set of angling problems special to saltwater fishing: intense glare, strong winds and spooky yet powerful fish. I set out with enough rods, reels, flies and leaders to last several lifetimes plus a selection of conventional weight-forward floating and slow sinking lines. Just before I left, I tucked a piece of tackle in my bag that would prove to be the Ace-in-the-Hole I needed to be a winner in this new game.

The flats were all I expected and more. Just outside my quarters were miles and miles of knee-deep water, raucous birds crying in the mangrove thickets and, when I learned to see them, dense schools of bonefish tipping down to feed, the exposed tips of their tails flashing in the bright sun like shards of glass. I couldn't wait to get my feet wet.

But my first day was humbling. The bonefish were far more skittish than I had expected, rarely allowing me to get closer than 60 to 70 feet for a cast. And, then, there was the wind. It was much worse than anything I had ever encountered in all my days of freshwater fishing. In preparation for this trip, I had practiced casting on

our local football field and felt very comfortable making long, quick casts into the wind. But all this seemed like a feeble gesture as I watched my conventional weight-forward line get blown around by the tropical breezes like a paper streamer. The only thing I could do consistently was drop a pile of line in the middle of the bonefish pods, then watch helplessly as the fish ran for cover, rippling the water like some tremendous rake!

Though I did manage better presentations when approaching the fish with the wind quartering at my back, I discovered another problem. The slick surface of my fly line left me out of touch with what was going on at the other end. And, when a fish took my fly—if I felt it—what with sweat mixed with sunscreen running down my arms onto my hands in the 98-degree heat, I often didn't have sufficient grip on the line to set the hook. As I returned to the lodge at the end of the day, I ran through all the possible solutions to my many problems, but could think of nothing new to try.

A cool shower and a fresh change of clothes did improve my disposition somewhat. Then, while rifling through my duffle bag in a desperate search for anything that could help, I found a box I had received just before leaving the States. In it was a fly line that was one of a new series of saltwater specialty lines Scientific Anglers had introduced. They called it the Bonefish Taper. The note that came with it said the line was "designed to handle problems bonefish anglers encounter" and would "improve my angling success." Well, it wouldn't take much to beat my performance on my first day. After quickly rigging the new line between curative cocktails at the lodge followed by dinner and a good night's sleep, I was ready to try again.

It was another beautiful tropical day. Bright, cloudless sky and those constant, powerful winds. As we headed for the flats, I pulled my cap tight around my ears. Today, it was still just me and the fish, mano y mano. But I had the new line and a new confidence.

I wish I could say that the line changed me from a confused beginner to the King of the Flats overnight. That didn't happen. But some very good things did that made the trip for me because of the Bonefish Taper line. First of all, I noticed this line is much more weight forward than a conventional WF line. That extra weight up front,

Jim Butler

combined with the shorter taper length and stiffer, narrower running line, helped me drive the line into the wind and made casting much easier.

What was really striking, however, was the line texture. Its rough, pebbly feel made my grip on the line more secure when setting the hook (which I was doing with greater frequency, I have to add) and when casting. I was also better able to detect takes in the first place. I first thought all of this was because of the line coating, but I discovered it was actually the braided monofilament core which you can feel through the coating. That textured surface also improves casting performance. Because the line "tiptoes" on all those bumps as it shoots through the guides, reducing contact and friction, you'll get increased line speed and improved shootability. The net effect of all these features on my bonefishing was simple: I began to take more fish. Not huge numbers, but at least enough to satisfy me that I no longer suffered from using improper gear.

Sure, I'm a traditionalist. Tradition is much of what fly fishing is all about. But go back to the old fly lines, even silk lines, as some would suggest? Never. The latest lines make our lives easier on and off the water with their low maintenance and high performance, and they certainly contribute to our fishing success. It's a rare occasion when I'll say this, but here goes: Hurray for progress.

Captain Earl Waters reviving a baby Homosassa tarpon.

Howard West

The Brittleness of Success

by Chico Fernandez

PROFILE: *One of the nation's most adept and innovative saltwater tyers and fly fisherman, Chico has become well known through his magazine articles for many publications. Many of his fly patterns are on display at the Museum of American Fly Fishing in Vermont. One of the few people ever to have landed a white marlin on a fly, he has also broken several records, including his 42-pound 5 ounce red drum that holds top IGFA rank on 12-pound tippet. He is now at work on a book on bonefish.*

*T*he trouble with success is that it can make you inflexible. This, I think, explains why even a knowledgeable, experienced angler may sometimes use the wrong fly line. He has learned that a given type of line works beautifully for him in several roughly similar situations that have superficial similarities but significant if subtle differences.

The following little parable concerns two old fishing partners, Fred Obdurate and Farley Hubris, who launched their skiff for seatrout one day in an area of grass flats two to six feet deep, with deep shorelines.

Drifting a flat while the tide was still high—about five feet—they were both blind-casting with 9-weight lines. Fred used a Wet Tip®, as he usually did on these flats, while Farley used the slow-sinking Monocore, as was his custom. Each used a short (six-foot) leader to keep his fly down close to the depth of the sinking line. Farley's Monocore took more fish—as well as the largest trout—simply because his fly stayed close to the bottom for the longest periods. Fred's sinking tip carried the fly down efficiently, but of course the fly gradually rose as he retrieved.

That afternoon, they fished an area of comparable depth, facing a shoreline laced with mangrove roots, stumps and fallen trees and branches. The situation looked pretty much the same to these anglers—but it wasn't. Fred cast his Wet Tip® with good accuracy, covering the mangrove edge with a weedless fly and also casting to any obstruction he happened to see. The line quickly sank the fly, and Fred would retrieve it a short distance, away from the shoreline, then pick it up and place it a few feet farther down the shoreline.

Catching trout and redfish, he was now outscoring Farley, who was still using his Monocore. Farley was losing valuable retrieving time—that is, fishing time. He'd strip the fly a few feet from the shoreline, but then, when he wanted to cast again, he had to strip another 20 feet through unproductive water to pick up and cast. Moreover, he needed several false casts each time to put the fly back where he wanted.

This little story emphasizes the importance of choosing the right fly line for a specific angling situation. The right choice usually means the difference in taking more fish—particularly bigger fish—or none at all. To make that choice, you must keep in mind the advantages and disadvantages of individual lines. Or, to put it another way, you need to understand the limits of all your lines.

The Wet Tip®, for example, has a big advantage when you're fishing a deep shoreline, potholes in shallow flats, or obstructions. Here the fish are looking for food at their level (or below) and won't follow a fly very far. You need to sink the fly quickly and, after working it for only a few feet, pick up the whole line and cast again to the next target area. Since most of the Wet Tip line floats, it helps you pick up without a lot of stripping. Nothing is better for this purpose—and I don't mean only in saltwater. It's excellent for largemouth bass around lily pads in relatively deep water.

But, if you want to cover a lot of water, blind-casting in depths of three to six feet, for example, a slow-sinking line is a better choice. With the Wet Tip®, the fly will start to plane back toward the surface during the retrieve, following the floating portion of the line. Soon, the fly is only inches from the surface instead of down where it should be. With a slow-sinking line, you can make a long cast (even against a stiff wind) and then fish the fly a few feet under the surface for the entire retrieve.

So, the next time you head out on the water, think carefully about what needs to be done and consider the qualities of the lines available to you. The correct match between the two will increase your angling success and productivity.

Chico and his world record Redfish.

Howard West

This hefty largemouth couldn't resist a Wooly Bugger and a slow retrieve.

Jimmy Nix with a braggin' size largemouth.

Bass: Getting Straight to the Point

by Jimmy Nix

PROFILE: *A pioneer of many aspects of bass fly tying and fishing, Jimmy regularly explores the far reaches of the fly fisher's world, including Belize, Mexico, the Carribean, Canada and the Rockies. His many articles describe the findings about bass behavior and habitat he has uncovered in his many years pursuing this fascinating species. In addition to his writing, Jimmy has presented his special fly tying techniques for bass in an instructional video.*

*N*ot so long ago, a gentleman called me about bass fishing. Like the rest of us, he liked to take them up top. There was nothing he liked better than fishing a floating line and a bass bug for those explosive strikes on top that only a big old bass can make. But he had a problem: he didn't take that many fish and, when he did, they weren't that big. He thought I had the answer.

It turns out that I did, but it wasn't the one he expected.

I explained that except for brief periods of the year there really isn't any good top water fly fishing for larger bass. It's because of the water temperature. Wherever you fish for bass, you'll always find them searching for water around 75 degrees. That's the ideal temperature for them. And, for most of the year, you'll find that range somewhere below the surface.

Needless to say, this gentleman was pretty disappointed with the news! But I told him I knew where to find the biggest bass in the ponds and lakes he liked to fish and I could teach him how to catch them. They were below the surface, usually around some structure, and he'd have to learn how to fish sinking lines to take them.

Many years ago, I was in the same situation as this gentleman: fly rod on top once in awhile, bait and spin casting subsurface the rest of the time. Then, I started experimenting with sinking lines for my fly rod to get my flies deep where the bass were and had some success. But I always had a problem I couldn't solve that convinced me I was missing more fish than I was catching. It had to do with feel or touch.

When most people think of bass, they have this stereotype idea that the fish hit your fly so hard the rod almost gets jerked out of your hand. This does happen sometimes, but not often. Usually what you feel is a "tap-tap-tap." Or, sometimes, it's a slow pull of the fly line caused by water flushing in the big mouth of the bass and out through his gills. When I used a bait or spin outfit, I could feel those light hits because I had fished a fairly tight line and had good touch for a pick-up. With my sinking fly line it was a different story.

What I discovered was the entire length of a conventional weight forward sinking line does not sink at the same rate because the belly section is heavier than the tip. This difference causes a big sag in your line as it sinks and this is why you miss so many hits. You just don't have the direct contact between your rod tip and your fly. The only way you can get rid of the slack is to strip your line in fast and this creates another problem. Except when bass are chasing baitfish in a feeding frenzy, you'll get most of your strikes fishing creepy crawly flies around submerged structure like logs, brush and weedbeds and crawling your fly down the edge of creek channels and points.

This problem was something I saw very clearly when I took that gentleman out on a private lake for some sinking line lessons. I put him where a feeder creek entered the lake, a spot I knew was loaded with big fish, and showed him where to cast his fly. Then I told him to count to 20 while the fly sank before he started to slowly strip in line. We both watched the line sink toward the bottom, but before he had reached 20, I noticed his line move to the left. He didn't see a thing and, because I wanted him to feel or see the strike, I kept my mouth shut.

That bass pulled that fly six feet before there was enough tension on the line between the fish and the rod tip to cause my student to set the hook!

For many years, I tried everything I could think of to solve this problem. I even cut back the tips of sinking lines till we reached the belly and fished this part! I did get a level sink and had pretty good results with these lines, but they were horrible to cast. And, I was sure I lacked the touch I needed and was still missing a lot of strikes. I am convinced that regardless of what species of fish you are after you just have to live with the problem of line sag as long as you use conventional sinking lines.

I still believe that's true. But, today, I no longer have the problem of sinking line sag because of a new line that I've been using since February, 1987. That's when the people at Scientific Anglers sent me a couple of prototype lines they called the Uniform Sink and asked me to field test them. After one fishing trip, I knew this line was exactly what I wanted: a sinking fly line that sank without forming slack and cast great. Best of all, the line gave me the touch and feel I need to detect a subtle take.

In fishing this line in all kinds of situations, now, I have discovered the Uniform Sink is even better than I first thought. It's the only line I've used that lets me feel my fly travelling over submerged structure like a log or a drop off. Bass just love to eat a fly sinking right in front of them and, when they do, I can actually feel them take the fly while it's falling to the bottom. With the Uniform Sink series of lines, I can fish bass in water four to 15 feet deep with total confidence that one of the sink rates can put the fly where I want it and I can feel the take.

So, while I don't recommend you throw away your floating line and your floating bass bugs, I do suggest you learn to fish for bass below the surface. That's where you'll find them—especially the big ones—most of the time.

Learning with Lines

by John Randolph

John Randolph

*D*iscoveries are to my fly fishing what yeasts are to bread. They vivify things. And they have a way of revealing themselves in such unexpected ways, almost as though someone had suddenly pulled a veil away to reveal a hidden truth. The veils keep falling, so my fishing remains satisfying. And, when I talk to Lee Wulff, now in his eighties, I have the feeling that he remains mentally young because he continues to discover new things. His fly fishing is like a walk in a woods after a spring rain: everything is fresh and new.

Let me recount some discoveries that have made a difference.

On one of my first fly fishing forays, when I was 12, my father instructed me to tie on a Mickey Finn streamer, cast it out and let the current take it downstream in the fast water.

"Let it swing and work in the current," he said, "and you'll get some hits and hook some fish."

He was a master of understatement.

The Green River in western Massachusetts was spring bright that May evening with fly catchers pirouetting in the air over the riffles to take the dancing mayfly spinners.

I stepped into the stream at the head of a nice riff and cast the bright-colored Mickey Finn into the flow. As it made the swing below me, the fly suddenly halted with a jolt. A bright silver fish leaped from

the whitewater and I fought in a 14-inch rainbow. I took five fish after that one, using the same "wet fly swing" on a floating line. The doors to fly fishing opened to me. I was bitten by the success bug.

What lessons did the experience give me? 1. Nothing works like success—fish where you can and you will catch fish. Your success will lead you on to other successes. 2. Keep it moving. Fish are predators—they expect to chase and catch their prey. Sometimes fish expect to see a fly drifting absolutely still—dead drift. But baitfish are prey for trout and other predators. When a fly moves like a baitfish, they respond to a killing impulse called a prey image. Use the line and fly to create the prey images and catch fish.

In my experience with the Mickey Finn, the line made the fly swing. It also may have made the fly appear to swim. As I fished more and more often with the wet flies, I came to understand that the fly line itself can be used to swim the fly in a variety of ways. Georges Odier of Aspen, Colorado, opened a door for me, revealing just how real the swimming motion can be to a fish.

Georges stood at the head of a riffle on Colorado's Frying Pan River, tied on a Western Coachman and put his floating line and weighted leader in the air. Brown trout worked here and there in the riffle, their dorsals and tails showing as they chased things. Something was on, a hatch of some kind, and the fish were excited. There were no bugs in the air.

Odier shot his line upstream and, after his fly hit the water, immediately threw a loop upstream in a fast mend. The fly quickly sank. By the time it had drifted 50 feet, the line jerked suddenly and Georges lifted the rod tip sharply. The rod bent deep and a fat brown trout surfaced and ran down the riffle. Odier stood in one spot and contiued to catch large brown trout, one after the other as though something had programmed them to his fly. It was uncanny. The way fly fishing should be but seldom is.

He explained it this way. By casting the wet fly upstream and putting the line ahead of the fly, you allow the fly to sink near bottom as it floats back downstream toward you. The fly sinks for several seconds in the heavy riffle water, then the floating line receives tension from the moving water and it swims the fly upward from the depths.

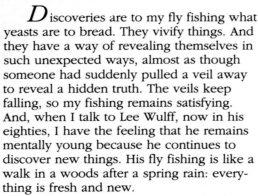

The Western Coachman moves the way an egg-laying caddis swims. Since the egg-laying caddis on the Frying Pan are fast swimmers, the trout must dash after them and grab quickly, impaling themselves on the hook.

What doors did Georges Odier open for me? 1. When trout see something real and edible, they sometimes abandon all instinctive caution and pounce on it. In fast-moving water, they must move quickly because the food is swept by them in a flash. They must make a commitment. That makes them vulnerable. Create the right prey image—one they expect to see where they feed—and you have a deadly weapon in your hands. 2. Lines can be used to swim flies in what we call a realistic presentation. While wet-fly techniques are old in origin, they remain a deadly way to fish. 3. Learn what trout feed on in each kind of water and each stream you fish and you'll be half way home in catching them. Matching the hatch implies knowing the foods the trout feed on in each individual river. Matching the hatch may, as in this case, be matching the movement.

A few months ago, I stood on a large, bathtub-like pool on the Grey River in southern Newfoundland and fished for sea-bright Atlantic salmon. A drought had shrunk the river's life-giving waters until the great polished gneiss boulders showed white like the bones of some prehistoric animal. In the plunge pool below the falls, salmon finned in the whitewater's sweet oxygen, a fish broaching here and there in the bubbles and foam.

I skittered a #8 Bomber on a floating line across the water's amber surface. A small grilse rose quickly and took the fly, leaping three or four times before coming to hand. During that first day of fishing, others took the fly, so I stayed with the waking, skittering technique. On the second day, fewer fish took the fly and, by the third day, they only played with the fly. They rose to touch the fly with their noses; they darted up to slap the fly with their tails; they planed up on their pectorals and drifted underneath the fly, then sank back to the bottom. I trudged back to camp that night mumbling.

Veteran salmon fishermen have long recommended low-water trout tactics for low-water salmon. On the third day at the pool, the fish finned diffidently in the comfort of their aerated surroundings. They

had seen enough of the skittering fly. I tried a smaller fly, a #12 in the same color, only dead-drifted this time.

On the second drift, a grilse sipped the fly, leaving a small hole in the tea-colored water. It was a nice day. And that evening in the darkness, I drifted my fly along a crease in the flow where the water slid easily over a boulder. The fly disappeared and I lifted. A grandfather salmon shot out of the gentle water and somersaulted. It ran well into the backing before giving up.

The lessons at the pool will always come back to me. 1. Salmon, like steelhead, like to chase things on the surface. They like to grab them sometimes, especially if the thing makes a small vee in the surface film and moves at just the right speed. 2. Salmon and other fish have no hands with which to touch and feel things. They grab them to investigate taste and texture. But salmon, like other fish, can't be fooled many times with the same techniques. They get wise to things. They must be shown something new and intriguing. They are as curious as little children but their survival depends on care.

Throw it out there and experiment. The surprises are the yeast in all of this. Trust me.

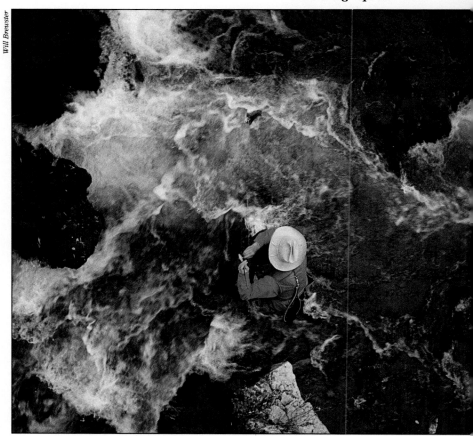

Will Brewster

Montana's Sixteenmile Creek holds some big fish in some tough spots.

Winter Steelhead and the Virtue of Patience

by Marty Sherman

PROFILE: *Having spent his early years backpacking and fly fishing in Alaska, Marty settled in Oregon where he soon discovered the joys of fishing for steelhead all year round. These magnificent fish soon became his passion and remain so today, leading him on regular journeys to the steelhead rivers of the Northwest. With his extensive experience in the fishing business—tackle sales, guide and tyer—Marty was well prepared for his duties as editor of* Flyfishing *magazine when he joined the publication six years ago.*

Marty Sherman admiring a rainbow from Alaska's Alagnak River.

When I opened my eyes, I saw a sag in the ceiling of my backpacking tent. I stuck my head outside and, in the faint morning light, I could see an inch of fresh snow had fallen across this wilderness landscape on the Oregon Coast Range. After putting on some fleece-lined pants and a jacket, I started a fire for coffee and headed to the pool I had hiked all this way in mid-February to fish.

A short hike through the woods led me to the pool I had seen and fished briefly on other trips. The last 10 days had been dry, leaving the river clear and falling slightly each day. Water flowed from left to right and the right bank was a gently sloping gravel bar. At the head of the pool, the water ran in through a turbulent, boulder-strewn rapids with a quick drop. The total length was about 150 yards with a slight right-hand bend until it found the tail-out and ran down a long, fast riffle for a hundred feet before flowing into a narrow bedrock gorge. The mid-section of the pool was four to six feet deep and strewn with rocks and depressions that broke the steady current. The tailout was lined with fine spawning gravel and it was easy to see in my mind robust wild steelhead paired over that gravel during late spring. The middle of the tailout also had several slots that looked like good holding water.

I had never seen a more perfect, more classic steelhead pool. At last, I had the luxury of studying it and fishing it for the next two days. No reason to hurry, just take my time and enjoy.

After breakfast, I gathered my gear and headed straight for the the pool. As I searched the bottom of the tailout in that early morning light, I couldn't see any fish at all. A crack of a twig to my left. Two bull elk moved quietly through the snow covered alders and I stood motionless as they passed. When I looked back to the water, something now occupied one of the tailout slots.

The steelhead was about average size for this river. Nearly three feet long and about 15 pounds. A thick, healthy fish. It looked very much at ease holding there in the slot, its tail waving slowly. After watching for about 10 minutes, I was confident the fish would remain and decided to try for him. I could use one of two presentation methods. Either an upstream cast with a nymph on a floating line or the traditional down and across with a wet fly from above on a sinking line of some kind. Since I could get close to the fish to see him while I cast, I decided to try a wet fly.

Cautiously, I eased into the river 20 feet below the fish and tied on a 1/0 General Practitioner. I knew the fish wouldn't move far to take the fly, so I concentrated on making accurate casts. My first cast—purposely placed far to his left—didn't seem to bother the fish at all. I aimed my next cast right in front of the fish just off to the side. After a dozen casts or more, it seemed apparent the fly lacked enought weight to get deep enough to interest the fish. If I cast any farther above the fish to let the fly get deeper, I would line the fish and spook it. So I decided to try the same pattern in size 3/0. I cast it just above the fish and gathered line while it drifted downstream. As the fly came within a foot of the fish, the steelhead bolted upstream into deeper water. Too much red and orange in such clear, shallow water.

It's always a disappointment to spook a fish so badly, but it happens a lot in steelhead fishing. So I decided to explore the rest of the pool and look for other fish. Toward the head, near the far bank in a hole beneath some alder roots, I spotted another fish. He was red, a small male that had entered the river much earlier. I thought it best to leave him alone to the task he soon had to complete. After exploring the rest of the pool without marking a fish, I returned to camp to relax and enjoy the woods. With coffee and a pipe, I rested under a cedar tree and watched the antics of two water ouzels and a flock of juncos. Before long, thoughts of steelhead drifted back into my mind and I decided to return to the river.

When I reached the tailout, I wasn't extremely surprised to see the spooked fish had returned. It was holding in the same spot. If I was to hook him, I knew I'd have to try something other than the large bright fly pattern and I would need to get the fly deep. The traditional downstream approach seemed the best alternative, but I didn't want to use a full sinking line. This line can create a problem: as the entire line sinks, the inside current can pull the belly of the line and cause the fly to swing at an accelerated speed, spoiling the presentation. To avoid this problem, I like to use the new Steelhead Taper V line. It has a 13-foot sinking tip that will get the fly deep fast and a floating section of the line that lets me control the speed of the fly.

I changed to my spool with the Steelhead line and moved up river, far beyond the fish's range of vision. I let out line at a 45-degree downstream angle, giving my fly the standard wet fly swing. It was apparent, though, that I would need to experiment with gaining depth. To do that, I cast more directly across and mended the floating section upstream, allowing the tip to sink the fly deep. Steelhead fly fishers have used this technique since the 30's and 40's, but it works so much better today because our fly lines float so much higher, cast easier and do their job so much better.

Eventually, I found the cast that got my line to touch bottom, telling me I was at the right depth. Then, I began to systematically cover the water using a slow cast-step-cast procedure downstream. I knew the fish couldn't see me and I wanted make sure he saw the fly first. As I moved downstream, swinging the fly, I could feel the line ticking bottom and, when the fish took, there was no doubt. Winter fish in cold water do not hit violently and this fish was true to form.

I felt a solid, steady resistance, a live throbbing. Then I set the hook. The fish boiled on the surface and raced 60 feet upstream in an instant. Because I knew it would fight the line pull from below, I let the fish run without any pressure at all. But, when he stopped, I bore down on him and the fight was on. Soon, it was apparent the fish was going to battle long and hard, so I pointed the rod tip at him and broke off. A wild fish like this is too valuable to jump through all the hoops just so we can touch them and say we won. I wanted to make certain this great fish was not harmed in any way that would prevent it from fulfilling its destiny.

That one fish was worth the whole trip into the back country and I think about that time often. I also think about how fortunate fly fishers are today to have all the new equipment—lines, rods and reels—that makes fishing for steelhead so much more manageable and pleasurable. Imagine, if you can, the winter steelhead fly fisher of the 40's and 50's. His only choice of rods was a slow action, heavy glass or bamboo. To sink his line, he had to treat it with paraffin and powdered graphite. What an effort to go fishing! Now, all an angler has to do is ask the fly tackle dealer to assemble the right outfit, pick it up and head for the river.

But, as wonderful as the new gear is, it doesn't guarantee success. The steelhead is still the same creature it was an epoch ago, just as fickle as ever. One day, you feel you have solved the riddle only to be totally dumbfounded the next day. What a successful fly fisher needs most to deal with the mysteries of fishing is lots of observation, understanding and large doses of patience. Like any other skill or sport, fly fishing ability requires time to develop. A good understanding of all aspects of the sport is the foundation to success, while the best gear in the world is an important tool to help you achieve that success.

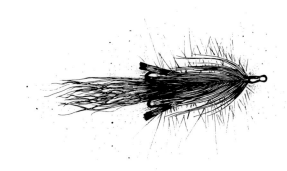

A Tough Trout in the Crowsnest

by Jennifer Smith

Jennifer Smith

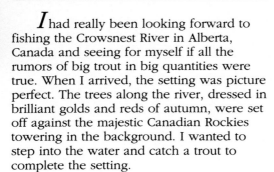

PROFILE: *Jennifer is a casting instructor and outfitter living in Bozeman, Montana with her husband and son. She enjoys sharing her ideas about fly fishing in articles she's written for many fine fly fishing publications and is currently writing a book for beginning fly fishers. When fishing, Jennifer never carries a measuring tape, a net, creel or watch. According to her family and friends, she has been this way most of her life!*

I had really been looking forward to fishing the Crowsnest River in Alberta, Canada and seeing for myself if all the rumors of big trout in big quantities were true. When I arrived, the setting was picture perfect. The trees along the river, dressed in brilliant golds and reds of autumn, were set off against the majestic Canadian Rockies towering in the background. I wanted to step into the water and catch a trout to complete the setting.

After a lot of hard work, I finally caught one trout. Not much considering the Crowsnest's reputation, but it meant everything to me. In the rain and snow, all the lessons I had learned didn't seem to matter this day. I had to stop and look at the water to see what it was trying to tell me.

There were no hatches or rising fish, so I threw every wet fly I had in the box from wooly buggers to copper nymphs. I fished them on the bottom and just below the surface. I twitched them, I dead drifted them. I swung them through the current, I cast them against the bank. I fished them just about every way I knew. My line stayed wet for nearly two hours without a strike before I noticed that, since I first set foot in it, the river had risen three inches and had gone from off-color to murky. It seemed certain the cold weather and increased flow had put the fish down.

I was preparing to leave for an early lunch when I caught sight of a trout rising against the opposite bank. The trout was feeding in the safety and comfort of an eddy. Eddies, which are really small whirlpools with a current running opposite the river's main current, are wonderful places for trout and difficult places for fly fishers to cast. You'll usually find them behind or in front of rocks or other obstructions measuring up to several feet in diameter. As water spins off the main current, it brings into the eddy aquatic insects, plants, small fry, terrestrials or anything that's loose and unable to chart its own course. And trout love it. In the calm of an eddy, they dine on their banquet at their leisure.

The trout I had spotted against the bank was clearly enjoying a nice brunch and I had to figure out how to serve him up a dish he couldn't refuse. I decided to wade across and downstream to get a better look at the situation without spooking the fish. The eddy was upstream on my left, moving clockwise. The trout was snug against the bank feeding sporadically at the edge of the eddy at the 10 o'clock position. I couldn't float my fly from above the trout because the current would push my fly away from him.

From where I stood, I could cast my fly to the 3 o'clock position and let the eddy current take the fly around the clock right past the 6 o'clock position and onto the 10 o'clock position right over the nose of that still unsuspecting trout with a big appetite. I began a series of presentations that followed this pattern, letting the fly drift past the trout, then rollcasting the line above the water and picking off the fly for another cast. After each cast, the trout continued to feed and, on the twelfth float, he dimpled the surface as he took my #22 parachute Adams.

Eddys are a great place to fish and unlike any other part of the stream. To be sucessful, you'll need careful planning and some patience. But the rewards are often great. If the fish are rising, determine what they're eating. If you want to match the hatch, that's fine. But I suggest you consider using a highly visible fly such as a Royal Wulff or Parachute Adams. Both you and the trout can see these flies. Use a leader no less than 10 feet, a light tippet no heavier than 3X and a rod no heavier than 7-weight.

You'll need a system that will allow you to cast accurately because you want your fly on the seam between the main current and the eddy current. This way, your fly will be pulled from the main current into the eddy current. Be sure to leave enough slack in your line so the fly can float freely in the whirlpool without drag. If the eddy is large, you may even have to feed line as the fly is carried to the far side of the pool. Be patient and stay alert. Trout who feed in eddys are notoriously picky and will take a long time to inspect items on the smorgasbord. If no naturals are showing on top, use this same technique to fish your favorite nymph, giving it a tantalizing twitch as it bounces and tumbles in the current.

On some days, when the water is high and off-color, fishing an eddy may be the only place to take fish which have moved close to the bank to escape the increasingly stronger current of the main channel. But an eddy is a great place to fish any time. It's always a challenge and can produce some great fishing for you.

Dealing with Those "Difficult" Situations

by Bob Stearns

PROFILE: *One of fishing's best-known anglers, Bob's articles and photographs have appeared in most of this country's leading outdoor publications. He is a widely acclaimed columnist for a number of magazines, including his well-known work as boating and saltwater fishing editor of* Field & Stream.

*F*ortunately for all of us, difficult angling situations don't always have difficult solutions. In fact, more often than not, the answer is reasonably simple—at least in principle if not execution!

I'd like to give you a couple of examples of some simple ways to solve a problem.

On a recent trip for bonito off the Florida Keys, I was trying very hard to catch one of these silvery bullets on a fly. We finally located a good school feeding all around the boat, but regardless of what pattern I tried or how fast I stripped, the best I could do was a few half-hearted follows. Even a noisy popping bug wouldn't work, though it seemed to create the most interest of anything I tried.

While taking a break on this steamy hot day without a hint of a breeze, an idea seeped into my sun-fried mind: somehow the noise seemed to hold the key to success. So I tried slapping the fly down on the water, leaving it there only a second before picking it up and, after a short backcast, banging it down on the surface again. Almost immediately I could see an increase in the swimming tempo of the bonito around the boat. The more noise I made, the more agitated they became. And, when I really banged the fly down hard, ripping it immediately from the surface with as much commotion as possible, two or three fish would rush to the spot and begin looking for the source of the racket.

After two or three noisy presentations to the same spot, all I had to do was let the fly sink an inch or two, then start a fast retrieve. Usually, it didn't travel a foot before it was attacked with gusto! Once I had solved the problem, I spent a thrilling afternoon wrestling 15 to 20 pound bonito on a 9-weight system. A real handful!

On another trip last spring, I was with friends fishing a clear desert lake full of big, chunky rainbows. We did well in the morning, but when things turned warm and breezeless, the hook-ups came farther and farther apart. By noon, the lake was a perfect mirror reflecting a pale blue cloudless sky and blazing sun overhead. Although not crystal clear, the water clarity allowed us to see everything in distinct detail on the bottom 12 to 16 feet below. It was obvious: the fish hiding in the vegetation below could see us just as clearly as we could see them!

We needed to figure out some way to

get our #18 nymph eight to twelve feet below the surface so it could be retrieved just above that vegetation. This was one of those situations where you wished you could fish your nymph on a 40-foot leader!

Instead, I used a 6-weight system with a Scientific Anglers Monocore line. The only disadvantage to this system is the slow sink rate of the Monocore lines. Since it is a relatively slow 1.8 inches per second (ips), I had to wait almost 90 seconds for the fly to get to the fish's level. But it was worth it! Once I got this clear-coated, nearly-invisible sinking line down deep, I started taking fish regularly. The rest of the afternoon was

extremely productive as I caught and released many of the nice rainbows that had earlier ignored the same fly presented with traditional sinking line.

If you prefer to use a shooting head system, this remarkable line is available in shooting tapers 6-weight and up. Personally, I really enjoy the lighter lines, especially when the wind isn't up, and, for me, that means a 5 or 4-weight system. If you want to make a 4-weight Head from a 6-weight monocore WF-6-S, just cut off 24 feet from the tip and make your shooting head from that.

I think these two examples show you

From popping bugs to silver spoons, steelhead see it all.

Howard West

that just one little key can make a big difference in catching or not catching fish on those days when conditions are tougher than usual. When things aren't going right, just take a few minutes to think about the situation and look for a different presentation method that will turn things around for you. And don't be discouraged. Even if it's a difficult situation, the solution is usually something simple.

Triumph Over the Philistines

by Lani Waller

PROFILE: *One of the world's leading authorities on steelhead fishing, Lani has written extensively for all the major fly fishing publications. He also owns a full-service travel agency for fly fishermen only—The International Angler—which he operates in San Rafael, California. A top steelheading guide and instructor, Lani was the logical choice to star in three tapes on steelhead fishing for the Scientific Anglers Mastery Video Series and has written a series of articles on steelhead fishing for the SA Fly Fishing Quarterly.*

Lani Waller bids farewell to another trophy steelhead.

*M*any years ago, on a cold, damp December day, a group of steelheaders stood in silence along a favorite riffle on Northern California's Feather River. Most of them were either out of work or possessd by The Fever. Perhaps, some were a little of both. All of them were grizzled oldtimers quite serious about their steelhead fishing.

I was the only fly fisherman in the line-up. I was trying desperately to keep up with the rest of them—casting my fly out into the cold deep currents and trying to keep it there—without much success. Every once in a while, one of them would hook a fish and the line of anglers would suddenly come to life, moving around in carefully orchestrated motions in order to accommodate the lucky steelheader who was hooked up.

The guy next to me looked about as friendly as a wounded bear and, for whatever reason, I assumed it was my moral duty as the only fly fisherman there to be as polite and good-natured as possible. (The thought also crossed my mind that I had no choice: I was hopelessly outnumbered and camped in the very Heartland of the Philistines.)

Well, I must have overdone it because finally the guy couldn't stand it anymore. Looking at my apparently useless choice of equipment, he discharged about half a cup

of chewing tobacco into the river, wiped his mouth clean with one swipe of his large hand and said in the loudest voice possible, "How come you guys never catch anything?" I immediately left to go somewhere else and think about it!

Through the years, I learned some valuable lessons and had some great days steelheading the rivers of the Pacific Northwest. But about three years ago, I received some new prototype steelhead tapers to test for Scientific Anglers and, in 10 minutes on the water, I knew my long range, deep water problems were over. I knew that with these lines I could put my fly in places normally appropriate for lures only.

Let me tell you about a trip I took this fall to one of my favorite steelhead rivers. I was joined by Trey Combs who was working on a new steelhead book that includes a chapter on this river and who wanted me to show him some of my techniques for fishing it. It was good to be with Trey, but I was in an awkward position. As his host, I wanted to make sure he got the best water each day; on the other hand, I wanted to show him how effective my presentation methods could be whatever type of water we covered.

The water was a little murky—14 to 18 inches of visibility—so dry fly fishing was out. Our best chances lay in deep water fishing with slow-moving fly swings. Since I planned to put Trey in "the buckets," (fishing the best spots), I had to look for resting and holding lies that would be off the beaten path and out of his way. This meant I'd be fishing very fast or deep water and, sometimes, a combination of both. I knew there would be steelhead in these places because some friends have fished them successfully with baitcasting gear. Such spots would be a perfect place to test the new steelhead taper lines.

The first day we fished, I hooked and landed three magnificent steelhead that I could not have reached without the new lines. What I used then is now called the Steelhead Taper Type V 13-foot Wet Tip line (a long name but well worth remembering!). The first fish was truly memorable. A bright hen fish of about 15 pounds, she came out of a pool we call "The Swimming Hole" because it's about 15 feet deep in places and you can take a real dunking if you wade carelessly.

The best fish in this pool lie along the right side of the tailout and there is only one way to reach them: wade along a narrow ledge that runs out toward the center of the pool. Because a wrong step will put you in 10 feet of water real fast, you have to fish from one spot once you reach it and, then, cannot change position to modify the angle of your presentation. So, there you are, totally immobilized in the worst position to make a good drift over the fish because, if you are a right-hander like me, the fast currents coming from your left create drag the instant your line touches the water. With strong currents and a casting target 80 feet away, mending is impossible. And, naturally, the fish usually occupy a very narrow, deep slot just ahead of two immense boulders. A very tough spot to present your fly deep with a slow, controlled drift.

As I waded the tightrope into position, looking at that dirty water, I thought about the many beautiful fish that my friends had hooked with their bright spoons drifted through that slot in front of the boulders. It would take a perfect presentation, but with these new lines, my confidence was high.

In testing the steelhead tapers before this trip, I learned how the design features would improve my performance dramatically. The weight forward configuration and radically dense tip created enough line speed to reach distant targets outside the effective range of conventional WF lines into the range of shooting heads. But, unlike a shooting head, I was able to mend the steelhead line to slow the fly's drift, putting me in total control. And, unlike the standard sinking tip line, the density of the sinking portion is high enough to get the fly deep enough in these situations.

The new steelhead tapers not only allowed me to do these things but also proved to be an extremely versatile line to cast. The feature of this new line that gives it such fishing performance is the hinging effect of the tip section. With the right technique—applying the power properly, then stopping the rod tip abruptly, you can "kick" the line tip to the right or left. And you can do it up to distances of 70 feet, giving you the ability to make curve and slack line casts that are impossible with conventional lines.

One observation, though: to make these casts, you will have to work on your timing and master the right combination of leader length and fly weight. Otherwise, you will be fighting a tailing loop and other casting difficulties.

Once I reached the middle of the pool, I was certain I could take a fish from this spot, but it wouldn't be easy. I needed an accurate cast to put my fly right in the slot. The cast also needed to curve to my right (a "negative" curve) so the fly would have time to get deep fast and not get swept by the current from my left over the fish. If this weren't enough, my casting target was roughly 75-feet away!

It took three tries to get it all together. Then, on the fourth cast, I stopped the rod sharply as I canted it over my left shoulder and the 13-foot tip hinged quickly to the right, putting my fly in exactly the right place. I watched the tip sink immediately and knew the fly was swinging right in front of the boulders. The line stopped suddenly and I set the hook. A beautiful 15-pound rainbow shot straight out of the water headed for the moon!

That was the first of many steelhead I've taken from tough spots with the new steelhead taper lines. Because I can put my fly in lies that other anglers wouldn't even try, I'm taking lots more fish when I'm on the water and enjoying the challenge of making those tough presentations. Steelhead are difficult fish to take, but these new lines have made the fishing of all steelheaders a lot easier and our presentations much more effective.

Brian O'Keefe

Get your fly deep, fast. . . they're down there.

Caveat Piscatore! Or, Preparation Is Everything

by Malcolm Jozoff

You've seen how 11 master anglers used a variety of techniques to solve a presentation problem they encountered fishing for most of the major species of fish taken on a fly rod.

Their expertise and success emphasize a major principle of this Guidebook: effective presentation skills will do more to increase your angling success than any one thing you can do.

But, lest anyone forget the importance of the one skill most critical to the success of any fishing trip, we've included a final piece on Preparation. Read it and weep. It's funny, it's terrifying. Every word is true.

Mal Jozoff

PROFILE: A perpetual amateur with the tastes of a professional angler, Mal has overpacked for fishing trips in Europe, British Columbia, Alaska, Western United States and the Caribbean. Somehow, there is always more adventure in one of his fishing trips than any six trips another guy might take.

I'm the kind of guy who prepares backups for his backups before a fishing trip. I pack spare spools for my spare spools. I take all the flies made in the factories of Bangladesh and Sri Lanka as backups to my basic collection from Kaufmanns, Anderson and Orvis. I select tippet material made fresh the day of my trip and, of course, every X-size that's legal.

You get the picture. I'm compulsive about preparation for a fishing trip.

So, when a friend and I booked a fishing lodge outside of Caracas, Venezuela in Los Roques, it was very uncharacteristic of me not to insist on sworn affidavits, notarized photos and a third-party inspection of the lodge. Somehow, the local booking agent had lulled me into a false sense of security with his reassuring, "Si, Senor, si senor. Perfecto, perfecto." I got off the phone with a song in my heart and plunged into the serious work of preparing my kit, rods, clothing, etc. I had such complete confidence in his choice of lodges that I ignored items six through 22 on my booking checklist—for the first time. And last.

The trip to Caracas was uneventful. My pile of gear and I were waved through the sweaty lines at Customs and passport control without incident. That I was everyone's best "amigo" was confirmed at every turn. As we stood beside the boarding gate, the thick tropical air smelled sweet.

Then our pilot for the trip to Los Roques appeared. Looking like the lead bombardier out of the Panamanian Strategic Air Command—black mustache, aviator glasses, enough rank indicators on his shoulders to make him Commander Supremo and a big gold tooth which I suspected served him as a compass during night flights—our leader explained that there was a "slight problem." After a lengthy explanation, it boiled down to one thing: he wanted more money "to fix things." I stood firm but uneasy. Not one red Bolivar more! The omens were definitely not good.

Soon, I could see the colors of the flats below as we made our final approach to Los Roques. Their beauty diluted my sense of foreboding. My previous experience with bonefishing taught me what prime bonefish flats looked like and this was definitely it. The stories about this island were the stuff of fast-growing legend and and, from the air, everything looked possible.

On the ground, we encountered a reality of another sort. With the Commander Supremo's assistance, our gear was loaded onto a push cart and we were soon following a small boy down the backstreets of the village past a mixture of houses with garbage on the lawn and chickens, cats and lizards scurrying in all directions. Destination: our Grand Villa. After what appeared to be some aimless wandering, we stopped in front of a very ordinary looking house. No boats, no dock. Just an average house on this average island. Our jovial hosts quickly escorted us through a small courtyard to a dark little room with four bunkbeds. The room reeked of Cat Smells and the floor was covered with a light coating of sand. We were going to be living in a litter box for a week! Not a good sign.

At least all our gear made it in one piece and, as we quickly unpacked, our hosts reassured us. Not to worry. Everything was the best. Food. Boats. Fishing. No problem. The best. We were anxious for a few hours on the flats, so with our tackle in hand, we marched down to the beach to meet our guides. They were very young, but I knew from experience that age was no correlation to skill. What really troubled me were the boats. Unlike any bonefish rig I'd ever seen, they looked more like pleasure boats with an awning. No platform, no place for the guide to stand in back and pole. Not a good sign.

Forty jarring minutes later, our guides cut the engines and we were soon standing in gin-clear water under a bright, hot sun. I had never seen more perfect bonefish territory. OK. We didn't have to be poled all over the place. Wading and stalking acres of bonefish-covered flats on our own would be great fun. The attempted "hold up" for more money in the airport, the culture shock of the village, the run-down lodge. It all seemed very far away now as I scanned the flats. We were here for the fishing. Our guide waved us along and we followed eagerly.

After two hours of wading patiently, no one saw a single bonefish. Not even the guide who spent most of his time picking conch shells. Then the rain came. It took no more than a few minutes of this afternoon squall and we were blasting back to the Grand Villa. As we dragged our soaked gear and fallen spirits into the bunkhouse, we discovered something we had overlooked in our initial inspection of our room. We had no window panes. It's only when it rains that you really notice what a significant contribution windows make! Water was everywhere and the freshening tropical breezes blew gusts of more sand into the room, forming a light crust over the tops of our beds.

Then things really got bad. My partner and I tried to liven things up before dinner with some old "war stories" from other fishing adventures and light refreshment from the island stock. Just as we started to rise above the day's disasters, we were hit with another trauma. Dinner arrived. A native woman brought a big bowl of cold rice, conch, onions and oil with lots of little snapper fish fried whole and, as we discovered, uncleaned. The only thing that saved me from complete collapse were the granola bars I'd stuffed in my bag and devoured before bed.

All night long, I tossed and turned in my soggy, crusty bunk, trying to escape the nightmares that floated through my waking and dreaming hours all night long. Like my stomach filled with the snapper and rice, I

Who do you know that broke two rods in one morning and still had rods to spare?

was having trouble dealing with the prospect of a week of days like today. I drifted in and out of sleep during the sticky tropical night, while the cats screamed and rats scurried across our bags.

The next morning brought no relief. It was if I had never been asleep. The nightmare would not end. For two more days, I endured but was diminished. Poor sleep, lots of sun, poor food. It all took its toll quickly and we felt very much abused at the end of another afternoon on the flats. We did find some fish and, sometimes, the fishing was good. That helped. I'm happy to report that at least my tackle preparation for the trip was solid. The flies, the tippets, extra rods and all the other gear were a perfect match for the conditions we faced. All of this made my time in Los Roques bearable, but never so thrilling that I could completely escape the miseries of our accommodations.

So, later that afternoon, when I noticed a small plane landing on the island, I found myself walking briskly back through town to the tiny strip. I introduced myself to the pilot (It was *not* the Commander Supremo) and asked if we could hitch a ride back to the mainland. "*Imposible*," he replied as he unloaded the bags of his passengers. Reverting to that great international symbol in all languages, I snapped a crisp $100 bill under his nose. "*Muy posible, senor*," he replied with a grin. In an hour we were out of there, bouncing back to Caracas and our flight back home.

Looking back on those days filled with mental and physical abuse, it's easy to laugh at the error of my ways. Never again will I let myself get smooth-talked into a fishing destination without proper investigation. Like locating fish, we need to select fishing locations where our personal needs are best met, where the standard of living is right for us. To ignore these needs is to greatly diminish our angling pleasure.

The days we have for adventures on the water—whether on far off exotic locations like Los Roques or our home waters—never seem to be enough. I think it's important to remember that because every time we plan a fishing trip we are laying the foundation for the success we dream about, setting the course for our destiny in the rare and precious days that lie ahead.

A supercharged bonefish takes a breather.

Howard West

Introduction

For over 40 years, fly fishing has been our only business. Our goal in everything we do is to increase the angling success and pleasure of our customers. Through the years, we've identified many needs and developed products for fly fishers all over the world as they explored the vast potential of our wonderful sport.

Today, we offer our customers over 400 variations of lines (we are the world's largest manufacturer of fly lines), a broad selection of fly reels and the most comprehensive fly fishing learning system on the market today (including the largest selection of instructional videotapes).

We are very proud of this tradition. Scientific Anglers teams—lab technicians, sales and service people alike—have drawn on their personal involvement with the sport and their professional talents to produce a growing line of innovative products like the Wet Cel® Uniform Sink lines and the System 3 reels. Because of our efforts, we provide the angler of the 90's equipment and information that is the best science can offer, tools that will create an opportunity for the highest angling success and pleasure of any generation.

Lines

We offer many options of floating, sinking and sinking tip lines because that's what it takes to meet the diverse needs of today's angler. With fly fishers traveling to more locations and fishing for more species than any other generation, we have developed fly lines that will perform in all conditions from icy steelhead rivers of the Northwest to the steamy tarpon flats of the tropics and in all situations from just below the surface of a quiet trout pond to the blue water depths just beyond the flats.

But, whatever fishing you do, you'll need a system of fly lines that best meets the situations you most often encounter.

Your first step is to choose the line weight that's best for the fishing you do. This will reduce your options for floating, sinking and sinking tip lines from over 400 to 12. Then, following the principle that each line with its unique function does something better than any other line, you can select the line that will get your fly to the exact depth you want.

This approach will work fine if you fish the same places all the time. But, most anglers see the need for additional lines as their experience grows.

Whether it's the pursuit of new species, exploration of new water or simply greater skills in locating fish and increased ability to present your fly, you'll want to add new lines to your fly line system. *Our advice is to buy one line at a time and master it before buying the next one.*

Building a system this way will greatly increase your range of effectiveness and your chances of hooking fish in any situation or condition.

Twelve 8-Weight Line Options

Floating Line:
- One of the Air Cel® Family

Sinking Lines:
- Wet Cel® Intermediate
- Wet Cel® I
- Wet Cel® II
- Wet Cel® III
- Wet Cel® IV
- Wet Cel® V (Uniform Sink only)

Sinking Tip Lines:
- Wet Tip® Intermediate
- Wet Tip® II
- Wet Tip® III
- Wet Tip® IV
- Wet Tip® V (Steelhead Taper only)

What color floating line do I need?

To answer this question, you must answer another question: "Is it more important for me to see the line or for the fish not to see the line?"

Our advice is to buy a high visibility color because they're a lot easier to see. Your choices are Sunrise Yellow (Air Cel® Ultra²) and Fluorescent Orange (Air Cel® Supreme). These lines can improve your timing on casting by allowing you to watch your line in the air. They're also great when conditions give you poor visibility, the low light of dusk or high glare of the noon day sun. And, if you're nymph fishing and watching your line for the slightest hesitation, they can't be beat.

If you're fishing super-clear, calm water to spooky fish, a low visibility, non-glare line in Olive (Ultra²)—a favorite for those New Zealand browns—or Gray (Bonefish/Tarpon and Steelhead tapers) are your choices. But, if you prefer an all-purpose line with colors in the medium range of visibility, you can choose from our floating lines in Buckskin (Ultra²), White (Air Cel® Supreme), Green (Air Cel®) or Coral (Bonefish/Tarpon Tapers).

OUR AIR CEL® FAMILY OF FLOATING FLY LINES

For that 10% of the time when they're feeding on or near the surface

This is where the revolution began.

Those old silk lines that floated so poorly for so short a time, that needed hours to dry and dress them? They disappeared almost overnight when we introduced the first Air Cel® line way back in 1956. After the success of this new revolutionary line, anglers told us they wanted lines that floated higher and cast even easier. So we introduced the Air Cel® Supreme in 1961. Our most recent contribution to the Air Cel® family—introduced in 1987—is the Ultra², the current state of the art in floating fly lines.

The first choice of fly fishers everywhere, the floating [F] line is the cornerstone for all fly line systems. With the core made of braided nylon and the coating of pliable plastic filled with precise amounts of 3M's patented hollow microballoons, to-day's high-performance lines have all the features our customers tell us they want in a floating line. Permanently buoyant, these lines float high for easy pick-ups, shoot smoothly through the rod guides for long casts and are made to last for seasons with little mainte-nance.

You can fish on or near the surface and, under the right conditions, take most gamefish with them. Floating high on the sur-face film and tapered to cast smoothly, it's also the easiest line to fish. Our most popular taper and the one we recommend—weight forward (WF)—is designed to help you make the right presentation for the fishing you do. For many of us, fishing on top—watching your fly disappear in an explosive strike or a delicate sip in the surface film—is the most exciting moment in fly fishing.

Today, we offer three different performance options in the Air Cel® Family of floating lines to fit the different needs of all anglers:

Air Cel®

When the pioneers who founded SA solved the problems of the old silk fly lines, they changed fly fishing forever. Scientific Anglers Air Cel® with its tapered, vinyl coated line that didn't need dressing to float was exactly what fly fishers needed. This line became the standard for all modern fly lines and the most copied fly line in history. The original modern floating fly line, this model has been improved over the years to float higher and last longer. Today, it's one of fly fishing's greatest values.

Air Cel® Supreme®

This model has even more microballoons to make it float higher and lubricants built into the coating to make it shoot farther than our basic Air Cel® line. Tests in the lab and on the water prove performance is comparable to the best the competition has to offer, but at a more affordable price.

Air Cel® Ultra²

The ultimate high per-formance fly line and our best seller, this line floats higher because of its for-mulation. The lubricants—they actually repel water—and the microballoon tech-nology in the coating cause it to rest on—rather than in—the surface film. This makes for easier line pick-ups and mending as well as better control.

Ultra²'s superior shootability is built into the line's total chemistry, not just a temporary surface coating added on. The coating formulation also contains an exclusive ingredient to reduce the

effects of ultraviolet radiation—the primary cause of cracking and fading—and other addi-tives to make certain your line will remain supple after seasons of heavy use.

Our Specialty Tapers for Floating Lines

Our standard floating lines are unsurpassed for handling a broad range of typical situations and conditions, but like all fly lines, they do have their limitations. Many anglers prefer to concentrate on fishing for one species. So, we make special high-performance tapers to help you master the situations and conditions encountered for bass, steelhead, bonefish, tarpon and salmon.

Bass Bug Taper

With a shorter front taper that helps turn over heavier, bulkier flies, even in strong winds, and a shorter belly for quick casts, this line is perfect for fishing typical bass structure and cover like sunken trees and lily pads.

With the BBT, you can easily shoot a cast of 50-60 feet to the target, retrieve it and, then, pick up off the water and, with one false cast, shoot it to the next target. As a result of this design, an average caster can now cover about twice the amount of water with the BBT than with a standard WF line.

Saltwater Taper

It wasn't long before the Bass Bug Taper found its way into the hands of saltwater adventurers who were looking for a line to turn over heavy flies in strong winds and also allow them to cast quickly to moving fish. With its overall shorter tapered section (head) it is an ideal line. So, to help anglers recognize the advantage of using the BBT in saltwater, we offered it under the name of Saltwater Taper (SWT) in the larger line sizes 6 through 12 weight.

Bonefish & Tarpon Tapers

Saltwater anglers were excited about the new SWT. They liked the shorter taper design because they could get off casts more quickly, a real advantage on the flats for cruising bonefish and tarpon. Yet, they couldn't get the distance they needed when the extreme tropical heat caused the lines to soften.

The solution to this "wilting" effect came during the filming of our *Fly Rodding for Tarpon* videos. At the insistence of our on-camera expert, Billy Pate, we tried coating a braided monofilament material he had used very successfully as a shooting line. The results were spectacular: not only were the new lines stiffer so they wouldn't soften in the sun, the braided core gave the small diameter running line a slight textured finish. Together, these two features greatly increased shootability, making it possible for a good caster to throw the full 100 feet of line with only one or two false casts!

No wonder that in just a few years, our Bonefish and Tarpon Tapers lines have become the first choice of flats anglers around the world.

Steelhead Taper

Our most recent addition to the Ultra² specialty floating line family, this line evolved from the success flats anglers had with the Bonefish and Tarpon Tapers. When some of our testers took these tapers to the Northwest and tried them on steelhead, they loved the line, particularly its shooting ability. But they found that the shorter head, which tapers so quickly into the fine diameter running line, made it difficult to mend casts over 40 feet.

So our staff, which includes a couple of wild-eyed steelhead fanatics, developed a special Steelhead Taper. It combined a braided monofilament core material—similar to what had worked so well in the Bonefish Taper lines—with a radically different taper design. What makes the new design so exciting is that its longer belly and extra-long rear taper make mending and rollcasting a dream, even at long distances. And the stiffer, smaller diameter running line makes very long casts—80-90 feet—easy for a good caster. Because cold weather makes the stiff, braided mono even stiffer, the same taper design is also available with our standard supple nylon core.

Today, our Steelhead Tapers have been called "the most remarkable development for fly fishermen in years" and have become the lines of choice for professionals on the challenging rivers of the Pacific Coast and the Great Lakes.

For the nearest Scientific Anglers dealer, call:
1-800-525-6290

Long Belly Taper

A longer belly section allows the experienced caster to carry more line in the air for greater accuracy and distance. This big line—105 feet in length—is the line for rollcasting and mending. Big river salmon and steelhead fly fishers will appreciate this taper design.

Salmon Taper

A 40-yard long double taper line designed for two-handed rods and spey casting. This line is ideal when fishing those big rivers with lots of brush and trees along the shore that prevent a normal backcast. Long a favorite with anglers in the British Isles, these lines are becoming increasingly popular in the Pacific Northwest.

Shooting Taper

Sometimes called "heads," they are the first 30 feet of a weight forward (WF) line. Rather than have its own belly section, the shooting taper is attached to a "shooting line," a fine-diameter level line. The ultimate in shootability and distance.

FLOATING FLY LINES
SPECIFICATIONS

Ultra²

Taper	Weights	Colors
WF	2-11 5-8	Buckskin, Sunrise Olive
DT	2-10	Buckskin, Sunrise
Bass/SWT	6-12 6-9	Buckskin Sunrise
Steelhead: Standard WF Stiff Core WF	6-10 6-11	Buckskin, Sunrise Gray, Orange
Tarpon WF	10-12	Coral, Gray
Bonefish WF	7-9	Coral, Gray
Salmon DT	9-12	Buckskin
Long Belly	5-12	Buckskin

Supreme®

WF	3-10	Ivory, Orange
DT	3-10	Ivory, Orange
Bass/SWT	7-12	Ivory, Orange
Shooting Taper	6-10	Ivory

Air Cel®

WF	5-9	Green
DT	5-9	Green
Bass	6-9	Green
L	4-9	Green

Buckskin   Sunrise   Olive   Ivory

Gray   Coral   Orange   Green

OUR WET CEL® FAMILY OF SINKING FLY LINES

For that 90% of the time when they're feeding below the surface

Soon after the Air Cel® floating line was introduced, fly fishers started requesting lines that would sink at precise speeds and, before long, we produced the first generation of Wet Cel® sinking lines. Through the years, anglers not only wanted lines that would float higher, but they also continued to ask for lines that would sink even faster. They got them.

The Wet Cel® family of sinking lines is the most comprehensive sinking line series on the market with 6 sink rates, including the slowest and fastest available. In 1983, we were the first in the industry to replace the lead in our coating formulation with tungsten, a substance that is environmentally safer and, because it's denser, enables us to produce lines that sink even faster.

The demand for these lines came from anglers who realized the severe limitations of fishing exclusively on top. They wanted to get their fly down where the fish are feeding 90% of the time and to keep it there. To do that, they needed sinking lines and, today, we offer two designs of full sinking lines, the standard Wet Cel® and the new Wet Cel® Uniform Sink series.

The big difference is *how* they sink.

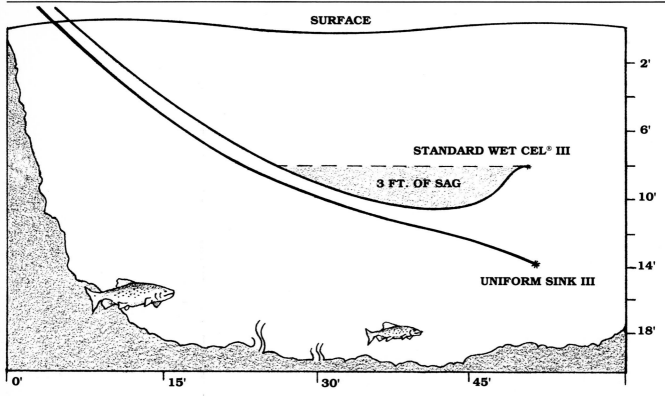

All traditionally designed weight forward sinking lines, like our Wet Cel® series, have more of their dense coating material in the belly section than the tip, causing a sag in the line as the belly sinks faster than the tip. The revolutionary new Uniform Sink lines, however, are designed with a tip that has a slightly higher density than the belly so there is no sag. This creates a more direct contact between the rod and the fly, letting you feel more strikes and get more solid hook-ups.

This difference is particularly important with lines of a higher density. The higher the density, the greater the sag. A Wet Cel® Intermediate line (sink rate: 1.25-1.75 ips) sinks so slowly that there is very little sag. But, when you're using the higher density lines, it's a different story: the sag is much more pronounced and a greater problem. It's in these higher densities that you'll find the Uniform Sink lines most effective.

To choose the lines you'll need, there's an important principle to follow: *each of our lines is designed with an effective range and, as you reach the limits of that line's effectiveness, you should switch to another line density.* Just be sure you choose the lines that will get your fly to the fish fastest and keep it there the longest in the situations you plan to fish.

Wet Cel® Inter-mediate

Sink rate 1.25-1.75 ips
Available only in the traditional design

Strong winds can push your floating line around on the surface of the water, causing your fly to move at the wrong time or speed and putting a belly in your line that makes hook-setting difficult. This line has a density just slightly greater than water so it will sink very slowly. Ideal for fishing wet flies, nymphs and streamers near the surface.

Wet Cel® I

Sink rate 1.75-2.50 ips
For fishing trout, bass or panfish over shallow weed beds or fishing just below the surface. Sinks slowly enough to permit a slow retrieve without sinking past the feeding level of the fish.

Wet Cel® II

Sink rate 2.00-3.00 ips
The best choice for your first sinking line (unless you have a specific reason for choosing another). Ideal for fishing lakes of shallow to medium depth (5-8 feet).

Wet Cel® III

(Hi-D®)

Sink rate 3.25-4.25 ips
To quickly get your fly 8-10 feet deep in lakes. A must for ocean fishing because the high density overcomes the buoyancy of saltwater as well as the effects of strong tides.

Wet Cel® IV

(Hi Speed-Hi D)

Sink rate 3.75-6.25
Handles extra-fast moving streams and lakes 10-15 feet deep. Its small diameter means longer casts into the wind.

Wet Cel® V

Sink rate 4.50-6.00 ips
Available only in Uniform Sink Series
Allows you to effectively fish oceans and lakes over 15 feet deep.
[Note: Unless you fish large rivers with even-flowing currents, a sinking tip line will be more effective than a full sinking line in stream and river situations because the floating portion gives you more control.]

Sink Rates:	Lines:	5	6	7	Line Weights: 8	9	10	11	12	13
1.25-1.75 ips	Wet Cel® Intermediate	•	•	•	•	•	•	•	•	•
1.50-2.50 ips	Wet Cel® Uniform Sink I	•	•	•	•	•	•			
	Wet Cel® I	•	•	•	•	•	•			
1.75-3.00 ips	Wet Cel® Uniform Sink II	•	•	•	•	•				
	Wet Cel® II (WF)	•	•	•	•	•		•	•	•
2.50-4.25 ips	Wet Cel® Uniform Sink III		•	•	•	•	•			
	Wet Cel® III (Hi-D®)			•	•	•	•	•		
3.75-6.25 ips	Wet Cel® Uniform Sink IV		•	•	•	•	•			
	Wet Cel® IV (Hi-Speed Hi-D®)	•	•	•	•	•	•	•	•	
4.50-6.00 ips	Wet Cel® V (Uniform Sink only)		•	•	•	•				

Specialty Tapers for Sinking Lines

In addition to our traditional sinking lines, we make sinking lines designed for fishing a variety of species and situations.

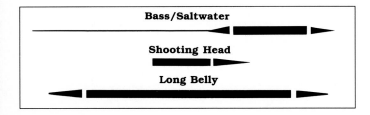

Bass/Saltwater

Shooting Head

Long Belly

Bonefish Taper

Sink rate: 1.40-1.80 ips
With a shorter head for quick casts, a thinner diameter that cuts through strong breezes and a stiffer, braided monofil-ament core, these lines are perfect for reaching out and sinking your fly to deeper feeding bonefish. As in tarpon fishing, getting your fly that extra foot deeper can sometimes make all the difference. Tough, abrasion-resistant coatings that won't tangle even in high temperatures that will wilt other lines.

Tarpon Taper

Sink rate: 1.80-2.00 ips

This line is for the serious tarpon angler who must be able to throw as much as 100 feet of line with a minimum of false casting. This stiffer line with its textured finish and short head is ideal for the long, quick casts you'll need to get your fly to deeper-moving silver kings. A heavier version of the Bonefish Tapers with the same durable coating and resistance to high temperatures.

Salmon Sinking Line

For those two-handed long rod fly fishers using the floating Salmon [see page 5] but wanting to fish a little deeper, we offer a sinking version in Intermediate and Wet Cel II sink rates. These 40-yard, slow-sinking lines may require an extra rollcast to bring them to the surface, but they will allow you to fish deeper more effectively.

Monocore

Sink rate: 1.20-1.80 ips

With a taper design similar to the Bonefish and Tarpon Tapers, this line is truly unique: it has a clear, single strand monofilament core and clear coating that makes it almost invisible. Perfect for those bright days on the flats when the fish are super spooky, the Mono-core has been nicknamed the "slime line" because of its slippery feel when wet— a real bonus when you need to shoot a lot of line.

As so often happens, anglers that have used the Monocore successfully on the flats have taken advantage of its characteristics when fishing for other species on other waters. Bass and trout anglers, for example, have found it an ideal solution for those lakes that are exceptionally clear.

DeepWater Express™

550 grain, sink rate:
7.00—8.00 ips
700 grain, sink rate:
8.00—9.00 ips
850 grain, sink rate:
9.00-10.00 ips

This is a fly line, not a lead-core line. Extremely flexible and tapered for better control. Won't kink, fray or break like lead core lines. Cut it to the right length "shooting head" for your weight rod. The fastest sinking lines made.

Shooting Line

100-foot spools of fine diameter level line to back up a shooting taper.

Shooting Taper

Sometimes called "heads," they are the first 30 feet of a weight forward (WF) line. Rather than have its own belly section, the shooting taper is attached to a "shooting line," a fine-diameter level line. The ultimate in shootability and distance.

Evolution of the nomenclature

We admit it. It takes a little study to get a sure grasp of the names of all our sinking lines. But it's really pretty easy once you understand the evolution of our lines.

The first sinking line was similar to today's Intermediate line. It was followed by the Wet Cel® II, then the Wet Cel® I and Wet Cel® Hi-D® lines. Next was the Wet Cel® Hi-Speed® Hi-D®.

See the problem?

To fix it, we've recently gone to a roman numeral system that makes it much easier to understand and remember our lines: we still keep the Intermediate name for our slowest sinking line, while Wet Cels® I through V are the numbers for lines with progressively faster sink rates.

SINKING FLY LINES
SPECIFICATIONS

Wet Cel®

Taper	Sink Rate (inches per second)	Weights	Colors
Wet Cel® Intermediate			
WF	1.25-1.75	4-13	Kelly Green
Wet Cel® I			
WF	1.75-2.50	5-10	Medium Green
ST	1.75-2.50	6-11	Medium Green
Wet Cel® II			
WF	2.00-3.00	4-13	Dark Green
DT	2.00-2.75	4-10	Dark Green
L	2.00-2.50	5-8	Dark Green
ST	2.25-2.80	6-11	Dark Green
Wet Cel® III			
WF	3.25-4.25	6-10	Greenish Black
ST	3.25-4.25	6-11	Greenish Black
Wet Cel® IV			
WF	3.75-6.25	6-13	Gray
ST	3.75-6.50	6-15	Gray

Uniform Sink

Taper	Sink Rate	Weights	Colors
Wet Cel® Uniform Sink I			
WF	1.50-2.25	5-10	Medium Green
Wet Cel® Uniform Sink II			
WF	1.75-2.75	5-10	Dark Green
Wet Cel® Uniform Sink III			
WF	2.50-3.50	6-10	Greenish Black
Wet Cel® Uniform Sink IV			
WF	4.00-5.00	6-10	Gray
Wet Cel® Uniform Sink V			
WF	4.50-6.00	7-10	Black

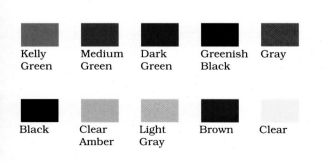

Kelly Green   Medium Green   Dark Green   Greenish Black   Gray

Black   Clear Amber   Light Gray   Brown   Clear

Specialty Tapers

Taper	Sink Rate (ips)	Weights	Colors
Tarpon Taper			
WF	1.80-2.00	10-13	Clear Amber
Bonefish Taper			
WF	1.40-1.80	7-9	Clear Amber
Monocore			
WF	1.20-1.80	6-9	Clear
WF	1.80-2.00	10-13	Clear
ST	1.20-2.00	6-13	Clear
Salmon			
DT (Int.)	1.50-1.75	10-12	Kelly Green
DT (WC II)	2.75-3.00	10-12	Dark Green
Shooting Taper			
ST (WC I)	1.75-2.50	6-11	Medium Green
ST (WC II)	2.25-3.00	6-11	Dark Green
ST (WC III)	3.25-4.25	6-11	Greenish Black
ST (WC IV)	3.75-6.50	6-15	Gray
Deep Water Express™			
	7.0-8.0 ips	550 grain	Light Gray
	8.0-9.0 ips	700 grain	Brown
	9.0-10.0 ips	850 grain	Black

Choosing Sinking Lines

To choose the lines you'll need, just remember that *each of our lines is designed with an effective range and, as you reach the limits of that line's effectiveness, you should switch to another line density.*

Keep in mind this key principle: as current speed, rate of retrieve or depth increase, so should the density of your sinking line.

The key difference in sinking lines is their individual sink rates which are measured in inches per second (ips) and listed on the fly line box. (Notice that the sink rates for any particular type of line varies by line weight. A Wet Cel® II for a 10-weight, for example, will sink more quickly than a Wet Cel® II for a 6-weight.) A simple guide to sinking line selection: the number of the sink rate (I, II, III, etc.) is about the number of feet your line will sink in 10 seconds in stillwater.

Your system should have lines with sink rates that will get your fly to the proper depth quickly and keep it there for the type of fishing you do.

8-Weight Sink Rates

Wet Cel
Intermediate	1.50	ips
I	2.25	
II	2.50	
III	3.75	
IV	4.75	

Uniform Sink
I	2.00
II	2.50
III	3.10
IV	4.60
V	5.25

Bonefish/Mono 1.60

Supreme Tips
II	1.85
III	3.25

Ultra Tips
Intermediate	1.5
I	1.70
II	1.85
III	3.25
IV	4.5

Steelhead Tips
III	3.25
IV	4.50
V	6.00

OUR WET TIP® FAMILY OF SINKING TIP LINES

For the best of both worlds

Because of limitations of both floating and sinking lines in some situations, Scientific Anglers developed a full selection of dual density (combination floating/ sinking) lines called sinking tip lines. The higher density front section sinks the fly, while the floating rear section allows you to mend the line and watch the motion of the line on the surface for indications of a strike.

Although the depth these lines will sink is somewhat limited by the planing effect of fast-moving water against the line, the control advantages they offer make them the best choice in many stream and river situations. In deciding which line is best for a specific situation, you will need to consider current speed, depth of water and rate of retrieve.

Scientific Anglers offers the largest selection of sinking tip lines with sink rates to match the fishing you do.

Air Cel® Supreme® Wet Tip®

High visibility belly for better strike detection. A choice of tip lengths allows you to fish the depth you want for a longer time. Floating section is Yellow.

Ultra² Wet Tip®

With an Ultra² floating section, you have the highest floating line available for easy line pick up and mending. The color of the floating portion is buckskin, while the 10-foot sinking tip varies in color according to its sink rate.

Ultra² Wet Tip® Steelhead Taper

If you've graduated from inland rainbows to their giant ocean-fed cousins, our Sinking Tip Steelhead Taper series will help you.

A 13-foot tip section lets you fish a specific depth longer than a shorter tip that can plane up in the current. Our new Type V with its faster sink rate makes this the perfect line for getting deeper faster in moving water. The improved taper blends the sinking portion to floating line over a greater distance, minimizing the "hinge-effect" that makes casting sinking tip lines difficult.

Available in three sink rates, including a new ultra-fast sink rate (Wet Tip V—sink rate: 5.5-6.5 ips), it's the fastest sinking tip line made. All three lines are 90 feet long to accommodate the long casts you will often need to make on steelhead rivers.

Floating section is Gray With this selection (Types III, IV & V) plus a floating Steelhead Taper, you can fish from top to bottom on any river by switching lines as depth and conditions change.

Note: Sinking tip lines are especially effective in moving water because only the front part of the line (10-13 feet long) sinks. In lakes, they are also effective down to about 10 feet.

Wet Tip® Inter-mediate

10 feet; WF-4-F/S through WF-13-F/S Kelly Green
Sink rate: 1.25-1.75 ips.
Most effective range: just beneath the surface

The 10-foot tip has a density just slightly greater than water which means it will sink very slowly and allow you to fish near the surface. Also, with the tip just beneath the surface, it will not be blown around by the wind, causing an unnatural dragging of your fly. Perfect for fishing wet flies, nymphs and streamers in streams and lakes

Wet Tip® II

10 feet WF-3-10 F/S
Dark Green
Sink rate: 1.50-2.00 ips.
Most effective range: 0-4 feet in stillwaters; 0-2 feet in medium currents

The 10-foot tip will gradually submerge a fly, making this an ideal line to fish just beneath the surface on fast-moving streams or still waters. A good line for sinking a fly ahead of a cruising fish in slightly deeper flats water. Or, for the bass fisher, try it with a popper and make the fly pop, dive and resurface with a start-and-stop retrieve.

Wet Tip® III (Hi-D®)

WF-5-13 F/S
Greenish Black
Sink rate: 2.50-4.25 ips.
Most effective range: 2-6 feet in still waters; 0-4 feet in medium currents

The best all-round choice, this versatile line sinks quickly, yet is easy to pick up and re-cast.

When choosing either 10, 13, 20 or 30-foot sinking sections, you should keep in mind two important principles. The longer the length of the sinking section, the longer the time your fly will stay at a specific level before planing up with your retrieve. However, the longer the sinking section, the more difficult it is to pick up and re-cast (the 20 and 30 foot lengths will have to be rollcast after retrieval to bring the line to the surface for re-casting).

Wet Tip® IV

Hi-Speed® Hi-D®

10 & 13 feet WF-5-10 F/S
Gray
Sink rate: 3.75-5.25 ips.
Most effective range: 4-8 feet in still waters; 0-6 feet in medium currents

When you're fishing the fastest moving stretches of streams—places where it's so fast you don't want to wade it—or when you need to go deep fast, this is the line to use. Also, perfect for probing those deep, dark pools most anglers pass up.

Wet Tip® V

Available only in Steelhead Taper design.
Sink rate: 5.50-6.50 ips.
Most effective range: 5-12 feet in still waters; 0-8 feet in medium currents

When you want to put your fly near the bottom in those stretches where the water is raging and ripping—the kind of water where only a ton of lead would get your fly down but so much you couldn't cast it safely—this line will do the job. Developed for Pacific Northwest steelhead and salmon rivers, this line's 13-foot tip will get to the bottom fast in fast-moving water. Or, if you're casting to banks from a drift boat and you need to get your fly deep fast, this line is a great choice.

SINKING TIP LINES
SPECIFICATIONS

Ultra² Wet Tip®

Taper	Sink Rate (inches per second)	Wts.	Tip Color
Wet Tip Intermediate - 10'			
WF	1.25-1.75	4-12	Kelly Green
Wet Tip II - 10'			
WF	1.50-2.00	3-10	Dark Green
Wet Tip III - 10'			
WF	2.50-4.25	5-13	Greenish Black
Wet Tip IV - 10'			
WF	3.75-5.25	5-10	Gray
			Wet Tip belly color: Buckskin

Ultra² Wet Tip® Steelhead Tapers

Wet Tip III - 13'			
WF	3.00-3.75	6-10	Greenish Black
Wet Tip IV - 13'			
WF	4.00-4.75	6-10	Gray
Wet Tip V - 13'			
WF	5.50-6.50	7-10	Black
			Steelhead belly color: Lt Gray

Supreme® Wet Tip®

Wet Tip II - 10'			
WF	1.50-2.00	4-10	Dark Green
Wet Tip III - 10'			
WF	2.50-4.00	5-10	Greenish Black
Wet Tip III - 20'			
WF	2.50-4.00	6-10	Greenish Black
Wet Tip III - 30'			
WF	2.50-4.00	6-10	Greenish Black
			Supreme belly color: Yellow

Kelly Green   Dark Green   Greenish Black   Gray

Black   Buckskin   Light Gray   Yellow

SPECIALTY TAPERS SUMMARY

When a passion for new challenges develops, the angler dedicated to the advantages of the right tackle will turn to the higher performance of specialty lines. These anglers have already discovered from experience that the more specialized the situation, the more specialized their tackle system should be.

Our specialty tapers, developed for specific species like bass, tarpon, bonefish and steelhead, are designed to increase your effectiveness beyond the traditional lines that may be part of your system. Owning these lines is a way to fine tune your fly line system and give you performance benefits

you'll appreciate when angling for new species in their unique environments.

And be sure to remember the unique characteristics that make these lines special: under certain conditions, these lines may be very effective when fishing for other species like using a Bonefish

Taper for bass.

(For complete descriptions of each of these lines, please refer back to the sections where the Air Cel®, Wet Cel® and Wet Tip® families—including the specialty lines—are listed.)

Bass Bug Taper (F)

Designed to make quick casts, an average caster can cover about twice the amount of water with this line than the standard WF.

SWT (F)

Using the same taper design as the BBT, the shorter head enables saltwater anglers to cast heavy flies into strong winds and make quick casts so necessary on the flats.

Ultra² Floating Steelhead Taper (F)

A new design featuring a longer belly, an extra long rear taper and a smaller diameter running line make it much easier to mend, rollcast and throw long casts than lines with traditional WF taper design.

Long Belly Taper (F)

The big line for big rivers, you can make long, accurate casts with this line.

Salmon Taper (F) & (S)

A double-taper line for long two-handed rods and spey casting.

Bonefish & Tarpon Tapers (F) & (S)

A short head for quick casts, but it's the braided monofilament core that keeps these lines from wilting in the tropical heat.

Monocore (S)

The clear, single strand monofilament core and clear coating make this nearly-invisible line perfect for bright days on the flats or lakes.

Deep Water Express™ (S)

When you need to get deep fast, this line will do the job without the casting and durability problems of lead core line.

Ultra² Wet Tip® Steelhead Taper (F/S)

The 13-foot sinking tip section lets you fish a specific depth longer.

Tournament Casting

If you ever get a chance to watch a fly casting competition, you ought to drop by. You'll be amazed at what these casters can do with their custom fly rods and lines all designed to perform very specific tasks.

In the late 70's, at the request of several of the

best amateur tournament casters, Scientific Anglers started work on a series of Tournament Casting Lines. It was another customer need that we could satisfy and, like car manufacturers who enter cars in the Grand Prix racing championships, we also felt we might learn some things

developing these lines that would benefit the design of our various standard and specialty lines.

Our SA Tournament Lines were first used in competition in 1980 and all winners in the distance competition used them. Using their special equipment, casters have been able to cast well over 65 meters (single handed) and 85 meters (double handed). That's 225 feet

and 280 feet respectively!

Today, all distance records worldwide* for the Men's and Ladies' Single and Double-Handed Fly Distance were set using Scientific Anglers lines.

* Listed by the International Casting Federation

Available in T-19, T-40 or T-120

For the nearest Scientific Anglers dealer, call:

1-800-525-6290

OUR FAMILY OF SYSTEM™ FLY REELS

Stopping big fish (our other business)

In talking to our customers about fly lines, we discovered something interesting: they kept telling us they needed a reasonably-priced, high performance fly reel with some very specific features. As hard-core fly fishers ourselves, we felt the same way. In fact, there were additional features, like a counterbalanced spool, that we wanted. We didn't see any reason why freshwater anglers shouldn't experience the same silky, vibration-free performance when a fish makes a nice run that the saltwater guys do with their expensive reels.

Our answer was the System™ One. In order to separate it from the pack, we built all the missing features into the best freshwater reel we could design at a price well below the higher priced reels that dominated the market. What pleased us even more was to be able to offer extra System™ One spools at about 30 percent of the price of the reel instead of the traditional 50 percent. Anglers like you have echoed their approval by making the System One among the most frequently seen reels on streams and lakes across the country.

Even though the System™ One reels have landed many big fish, our salmon, steelhead and saltwater friends asked for bigger capacity reels with a powerful drag. Our international design team came up with the System™ Two series which brought "stop a train" disc drag performance within the price range of the not so rich and famous. And the fly reel market hasn't been the same since.

Our latest evolutionary step, the System™ 3, is really even more of a leap. Simply stated, it features the smoothest drag you can buy at any price. Its new patented drag design radically departs from the age-old cork to metal systems. And, further breaking traditions—at least ours—at about $700, it's not all that affordable. Just difficult to live without if you fish for the big, fast and the mean.

Why? Whatever the product, we are driven to produce the very best and we think the System™ 3 is the ultimate reel. One field tester called the 3 "an unfair advantage...like being connected to the fish by a laser." It's certainly not intended for everyone, yet if you are fishing for the quick and powerful species, like tarpon, you'll need all the edge you can get.

System™ One
Unusually high performance at an affordable price

Talk about high performance. A friend of ours landed a 43-pound Alaskan King salmon with a model 789, while on the same trip, two of his buddies "blew up" more expensive reels. With a strong full frame construction, adjustable click drag that really works, exposed spool rim for extra drag, counter-balanced spool, tough cast aluminum alloy body and spool, each with a durable baked enamel finish, and very affordable extra spools, you can't buy a more dependable or higher performing freshwater reel for less.

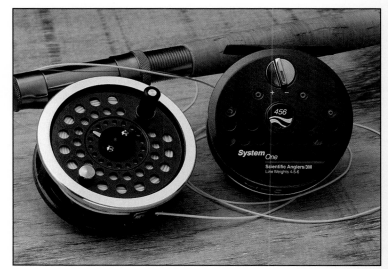

Model	For Line Weights	Spool Diameter and Width	Backing Capacity (20 lbs)	Reel Weight
456	4, 5 or 6	3-1/4" x 13/16"	85 yards (WF-6-F)	4.6 oz.
789	7, 8 or 9	3-7/16" x 7/8"	85 yards (WF-6-F)	4.6 oz.

System™ Two-L

For those who can't say "trout" without thinking "big"

This reel's big brother, the System Two, changed forever the standard of performance steelheaders and saltwater fans expected from a reel. The only complaint was the System™ Two was too big and overpowered for most trout. So the challenge was to design a down-sized drag system sensitive enough to hold onto lightning-quick rainbows on 6X, yet with enough muscle to put the heat on a summer-run steelhead.

By enlisting the same design team that created the System™ Two and focusing their efforts on stopping trout not trains, we came up with a whisper-smooth single caliper disc drag system that's second to none. Around it, we wrapped all the features anglers like so well in the System™ One and Two, like a counter-balanced spool with an exposed rim for "just in time" extra drag pressure. And, of course, modestly priced extra spools so you can't afford to be without that extra Wet Tip® or Uniform Sink line that will get your fly deep when the "big cruisers" aren't feeding near the surface.

Model	For Line Weights	Spool Diameter and Width	Backing Capacity (20 lbs)	Reel Weight
45-L	4 or 5	2-15/16" x 5/8"	85 yds (WF-5-F)	4.7 oz.
56-L	5 or 6	2-15/16" x 3/4"	110 yds (WF-6-F)	4.8 oz.
67-L	6 or 7	2-15/16" x 7/8"	125 yds (WF-7-F)	5.0 oz.
78-L	7 or 8	2-15/16" x 1"	150 yds (WF-8-F)	5.2 oz.

System™ Two-LC

All the goodies except the disc drag

The LC is for all the trout anglers who asked for a smaller diameter trout reel than the System One, yet with a finely adjustable click drag instead of a disc. The System™ Two 56 LC model, for example, is 2-15/16" in diameter, a full 1/4" smaller than a System™ One, yet it holds 30 percent more backing with a WF-6-F line and is 1/3 oz. lighter.

Like the disc drag model, the System Two-LC has an exposed spool rim for applying extra drag, a counter-balanced spool, a comfortable size handle and inexpensive spare spools. Although there are many nice small diameter click drag reels on the market, our customers say the LC reel feels right and sounds more like a fine trout reel should.

Model	For Line Weights	Spool Diameter and Width	Backing Capacity (20 lbs)	Reel Weight
45 LC	4 or 5	2-15/16" x 5/8"	85 yds (WF-5-F)	4.3 oz.
56 LC	5 or 6	2-15/16" x 3/4"	110 yds (WF-6-F)	4.5 oz.
67 LC	6 or 7	2-15/16" x 7/8"	125 yds (WF-7-F)	4.6 oz.
78 LC	7 or 8	2-15/16" x 1"	150 yds (WF-8-F)	4.8 oz.

System™ Two
"Train-stopping power"

This is the reel that has changed how serious anglers measure fish-stopping power. In just four years, the System™ Two has become the most popular disc drag reel in the world and, if imitation is flattery, our reel designers did their job well. Proven on monster steelies in British Columbia, the speedy bones' of Christmas Island and the powerful tarpon of Florida, this reel can do it all. (One happy angler showed us on video how he "crushed" a mean 160-pound Homosassa tarpon with a System™ Two in under 45 minutes!)

The heart of the System Two is the sophisticated disc brake drag system. Stainless steel calipers with automotive-type brake pads and a polished stainless steel disc make this drag system smooth, powerful and beautifully uncomplicated. With a finely adjustable drag from 0-7 pounds and a generously wide exposed spool rim for selectively applying just the right amount of additional pressure to back up a sulking fish, you have maximum control.

Each model is designed with plenty of backing capacity for specific species.

At 3-1/2 inches in diameter and capacity for up to 240 yards of 20-lb. backing with a WF-8-F, the 78 model is ideal for strong running steelhead, Atlantic salmon and other species from bluefish to bonefish. For those who use 9-weight lines or want more capacity, the 3-3/4 inch diameter Model 89 holds 330 yards of 20-lb. backing and features a uniquely comfortable rubber handle to prevent tired and bruised fingers during those epic battles with everything from King salmon to big permit.

Our largest model, the 1011, fits the need for medium-heavy saltwater fishing from big barracudas to tarpon and everything in between. At only 8.8 ounces, it's light in weight for a big capacity reel and you don't have to worry about not having enough stopping power.

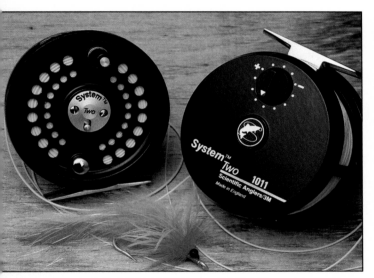

Model	For Line Weights	Spool Diameter and Width	Backing Capacity (20 lb)	Reel Weight
67	6 or 7	3-1/2" x 3/4"	150 yards WF-7-F	6.9 oz.
78	7 or 8	3-1/2" x 1"	240 yards WF-8-F	7.2 oz.
89	8 or 9	3-3/4" x 1"	330 yards WF-9-F	8.5 oz.
1011	10 or 11	3-3/4" x 1-3/16"	390 yards WF-11-F	8.8 oz.

Buying a Fly Reel

Despite appearances, all reels are not created equal. Sometimes, the needs of the angler are overshadowed by those of the penny-pinching accountants and overzealous engineering types.

First, you'll need to decide the size of the fly lines and the amount of backing you need for the fishing you plan to do. Next, you'll want to make sure the weight of the reel balances with your rod.

That's the simple stuff. There are some other, less obvious but no less important criteria to consider.

Some reels promote their lightness as if that were everything. But you have to consider what the manufacturer did to make the reel so light. The difference in a 3 and 4 ounce reel may sound big, but when you load backing and line on both reels, you probably can't tell the difference. And you have to consider what they did to eliminate 25 percent of the weight. "Where," you might well ask, "did the missing ounce of metal come from?"

To find out if a reel's durability has been designed away, you can check a couple of things. You can test the cage frame and spool by applying light pressure from your forefinger and thumb. If they flex, let someone else buy the reel.

The other critical feature is the drag. This is what separates high-performance reels from the also-rans. There are three basic types of drags: click, disc and "O" Ring.

Click: If you're a freshwater fly fisher who won't be playing any "line burners," then buy a quality reel with a click drag. Its only limitation is it can't smoothly produce much resistance to strong running fish.

(continued on page 103)

System™ 3

the search for excellence. . . our obsession

When it's just you and the biggest, fastest, meanest thing that swims, this is the reel to have. Many reel makers offer quality "big game" reels. They all seem to be precision-machined from solid bars of T-6061 aluminum to whisker-thin tolerances and anodized to a beautiful polished finish. The 3 is great-looking, too, but beauty is truly only surface-deep when you are hooked onto a Cuba-bound tarpon. It's the drag that separates the good reels from the great. After three years of testing and refining, we feel the

System™ 3—with the smoothest performance drag system you can buy at any price—is the Ultimate Fly Reel.

For decades the accepted means of developing drag force was pushing cork against metal. Some designs use oil-impregnated cork or simply lube its surface. Others add teflon or leather discs. Regardless of the material used, they are basically the same design and perform about equally as well. Typically, with a big running fish, this friction type design generates a lot of heat which can cause

the drag force to vary. In addition, when a fish stops and then quickly surges off again, it takes considerably more force to break the spool free (spool start up inertia) than it does to keep the spool spinning (running drag). In practical terms, what this means is you have to set your drag lighter in order to protect your tippet in the anticipation of a sudden burst, thus prolonging the fight.

We thought there might be a better way and, with these factors in mind, we began looking for a more efficient drag design. The search lead us to Herman

Voss, an avid South Florida fly rodder and mechanical engineer. Teaming Voss up with the Scientific Anglers designers, we came up with a totally new and patented drag concept based on using "O" rings instead of cork: two lubricated and specially-formulated polyfluoroelastomer "O" rings (1.23 in diameter and .103 inches thick) positioned on both sides of a stainless steel ratchet disc which in turn is sandwiched between two movable outer housings.

As you turn up the drag, the two outer hous-

Model	For Line Weights	Spool Diameter and Width	Backing Capacity	Reel Weight
1112	11 or 12	3-15/16"	(30 lb) 370 yds WF-12-Tarpon Taper (20 lb) 525 yds WF-12-Tarpon Taper	10.2 oz.
Extra spools available.				

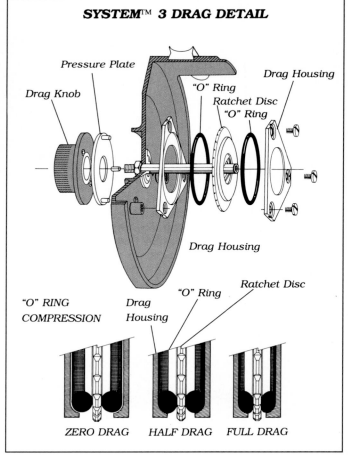

SYSTEM™ 3 DRAG DETAIL

Drag Knob — Pressure Plate — "O" Ring — Ratchet Disc — "O" Ring — Drag Housing

Drag Housing

"O" RING COMPRESSION — Drag Housing — "O" Ring — Ratchet Disc

ZERO DRAG   HALF DRAG   FULL DRAG

ings are pushed together, compressing the "O" rings and increasing the drag force on the ratchet disc. Because the "O" ring and the stainless steel disc have very smooth surfaces and are both coated in a high temperature lubricant, there is very little friction and, consequently, less start-up force required to start the spool turning against the drag. So you can use more drag force against a fish without worrying about "breakaway inertia." In addition, the spool has a wide exposed rim and a very comfortable, non-slip rubber handle that feels just as nice after two hours of "poon wrestling" as it does out of the box.

Since the "O" ring drag is nearly a sealed system, dirt and grit won't affect its smoothness and you can soak it in water without losing any drag force. This means the "O" ring system won't become sticky with age and requires very little maintenance. In fact, all the parts in the entire reel are either stainless steel, deep anodized aluminum or made of a non-corrosive material.

Designed with plenty of metal in the high-abuse places, like the exposed spool rim, the System™ 3 model 1112 is comfortably light at 10.2 oz., yet holds 370 yards of 30-pound backing and a full 100 foot WF-12-F Tarpon Taper. We've also given special attention to another problem area for many Big Game reels: the reel foot. Machined from solid brass and chrome-plated, ours is dove-tailed and hand-fitted into the frame. And, for additional security, there's a small retaining screw that's not subjected to stress.

(Buying a Fly Reel, cont.)

Available in our System™ One and System™ Two LC reels.

Disc: A properly designed disc drag can generate many times more drag force than a click drag. What determines smoothness and durability are the materials used for the drag. Today, the most dependable disc drags are no longer made of cork but rather use metal calipers with special brake pads that will stand up to the friction-generated heat of a long run and won't dry out over time.

Available in our System™ Two and System™ Two-L reels.

O-Ring: Newly patented for exclusive use in our System™ 3 reels, our field testers say this is the ultimate drag system. Its unique and wonderfully uncomplicated design features two specially formulated Space Age material O-Rings bathed in high-temperature resistant lubricants that are squeezed against a special clutch housing to produce a powerful yet smooth, steady pressure with little heat. This drag also features very low start-up enertia: this means when a fish makes a sudden burst, you won't have to worry because it takes very little force to start the spool moving against the drag. Powerful yet widely adjustable through the entire drag range and even unaffected by a good dunking, this is the ideal drag for serious saltwater fly fishers.

Available only in our System™ 3 reel.

For the nearest Scientific Anglers dealer, call:
1-800-525-6290

ACCESSORIES

A system of individual tackle components designed to work together—a balanced fly fishing system—will help you present your fly correctly in a variety of situations and make your casting a lot more fun. This principle was pioneered by Scientific Anglers and still guides everything we do. It influences all the products we make, including fly fishing accessories.

System™ Backing

This part of your system is important for several reasons. It lets your line form larger coils on the spool, which dramatically reduces annoying coils, and lets you recover line faster. Backing's main job, however, is to give you added insurance when playing a long running fish.

Because it's the thinnest you can buy, Scientific Anglers backing lets you get more on the reel for added protection and, because it's made of low-stretch Dacron®, it won't damage your reel when wound in under the pressure of a big fish.

Available in 30# test for use in saltwater and abrasive conditions, 20# test for most applications and 12# test for use with lighter tippets or situations where lower drag in the water and greater capacity are important. Available in spools of 100, 400 (four spools joined), 1,000 and 3,000 yards.

("Dacron" is a registered trademark of Du Pont®)

System™ Tapered Leaders and Tippets

An important link in your system, hi-performance leaders and tippets should match your fly line and the flies you use for most effective casting. Your leader should turn your fly over easily, transfer the energy from the fly line smoothly and allow the fly to drift naturally.

Designed in tapered "steps," our System Leaders are made of nylon copolymer (a special type of monofilament) formulated to provide the characteristics of a high-performance leader.

They have the right blend of stiffness and flexibility to help you make a natural presentation of your fly and have low water absorbtion for consistent line and knot strength. Both our leaders and tippets are also formulated to stretch so they can absorb sudden shocks from hook-setting or bolting fish without breaking and to resist abrasion that can come from rocks or teeth and cause small nicks that can weaken your system.

Leaders available in 14 strengths, 5 butt diameters and 4 lengths. Tippets available in 25-meter spools in diameters 0X to 8X. They give you the variety of strength and lengths you need to match the fishing you do.

SYSTEM KNOTLESS TAPERED LEADERS										Extra Heavy Tapered Leaders				
Specifications	0X	1X	2X	3X	4X	5X	6X	7X	8X					
Tip Diameter	.011	.010	.009	.008	.007	.006	.005	.004	.003	.011	.012	.013	.014	.015
Butt Diameter	.021	.021	.021	.021	.021	.021	.017	.015	.013	.023	.023	.023	.023	.023
Test LB	10	9	7	6	5	4	3	2	1	10	12	14	15	16
6 ft														
7-1/2 ft														
9 ft														
12 ft														
Heavy butt 9 ft														
Heavy butt 12 ft														

System™ Fly Boxes

Our **System™ Fly Boxes** have been newly-designed to provide some additional features our customers have requested and are now made in the USA. You'll find a strong, continuous hinge on the back with tapered ends so its easy to get in and out of tight pockets. A recessed lanyard tab on one corner has been added so you can attach the box to a belt or vest for easy access.

On both sides of the small boxes and on one side of the medium, we've included fine-celled flat foam to hold those small flies and barbless hooks. The larger boxes use a coarse foam in flat and ripple textures to hold

larger flies securely even in high winds and rain. The big advantage of using foam to hold flies over boxes using the "compartment" style is fly selection. With our System™ Boxes you can see all your flies at a glance, compare sizes and remove them quickly. No more poking around those piles of matted flies!

The other great thing about our rustproof boxes is they are ultra light-weight and virtually indestructible. Even if you drop one overboard or into the creek, the foam acts as built-in flotation so you won't lose them.

The System™ Boxes come in five models to fit all your fly storage needs:

Getting Started. . . Easier

Fly Fishing System™

Other accessories to take care of basic angling needs include:

A Fly Fishing System pack to take the guess-work out of choosing tackle for bass, panfish

and trout for those new to the sport. Each pack comes complete with a Concept WF floating line, 7 1/2-foot tapered System Leader and 100 yards of System Backing all perfectly balanced for easy casting.

Concept®

Developed especially for those new to the sport, the taper design of these lines can actually help counter-act some of the common casting problems. Available in both floating and sinking lines in the most popular weights and tapers. Floating lines come in Yellow so they're easy to follow in the air to check your casting loop or on the water so you can track your line drift. Sinking lines come in Green.

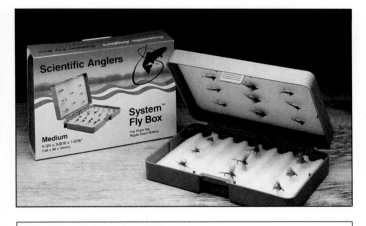

SYSTEM™ FLY BOXES	
Small (flat/flat)	3-1/2 x 2-1/2 x 1"
Medium (flat/ripple)	5-3/4 x 3-9/16 x 1-5/16"
Medium (flat/flat)	5-3/4 x 3-9/16 x 1-5/16"
Large (flat/ripple)	8-3/8 x 4-1/2 x 1-3/8"
Large (flat/flat)	8-3/8 x 4-1/2 x 1-3/8"

Publications

In the early 70's, we re-dedicated ourselves to removing the myth and mystery that made fly fishing so difficult for beginners and frustrating for all of us who wanted to become accomplished fly fishers. Our first step was to introduce our Scientific Anglers *Fly Fishing Handbook* series, which at our readers' requests eventually evolved into the SA *Fly Fishing Quarterly*.

Later, in the 80's, we discovered the learning power of videotapes and, in five short years, produced 18 videotapes on trout fishing, steelheading and fly rodding for tarpon. By combining the instructional capabilities of both the written and visual media, we have developed a fun and systematic approach to fly fishing that dramatically decreases the start-up time for new anglers and shortens the learning curve for mastering even the most complex techniques.

We hope you enjoy our publications and videotapes and encourage you to send us your ideas for new ones.

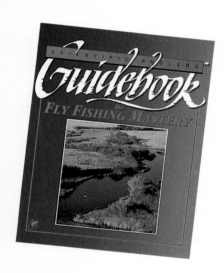

A Guidebook to Fly Fishing Mastery

Contains some of the most in-depth information ever written on fly fishing. This 100-page book will teach you to see with "expert" eyes and describes the basic principles you'll need to achieve angling success. Using Scientific Anglers Formula for Success, you'll learn how to locate fish in saltwater and freshwater, how to choose and use the tackle you'll need for whatever species you pursue and how to prepare yourself to fully enjoy your time on the water. Also includes over a dozen articles by master anglers who explain how they use the Formula for Success to solve angling riddles. (Available at tackle shops and direct from Scientific Anglers. $9.95.)

Fly Fishing Made Easy

handbook is a starting point for beginners and a refresher course for more advanced anglers. Leading fly fishing instructors give step-by-step diagrams that lead you through equipment selection, assembly and casting basics. Also, you'll get the basics on reading the water, understanding hatches and presentation methods for taking trout, bass and panfish. (Available from tackle dealers or direct from Scientific Anglers at $2.95.)

A Fly Fisher's Pocket Guide (48 pages) helps you assemble your equipment without frustration. Includes advice on how to build a balanced tackle system and detailed descriptions of how to tie the knots for the fishing you do. (Free: packed inside each SA line box.)

Fly Fishing Quarterly

Features the newest, most innovative ideas in fly fishing. In-depth articles, columns and series focus on a wide range of topics, including presentation strategies and techniques for all species and solving common angling problems. Directed to the dedicated fly fisher who seeks a source of sophisticated, complete information that will be of practical help in improving their skills. Includes dozens of spectacular angling photos and illustrations by leading outdoor artists. (Available at tackle shops, newsstands and by subscription. $3.50.)

Subscriptions are available for one year ($12.95) and two years ($21.95).

Make checks payable to Scientific Anglers *Fly Fishing Quarterly* and mail to:

Scientific Anglers *Fly Fishing Quarterly* Subscription Department P.O. Box 3000 Denville, N.J. 07834-9863 Dept. SAF

106

LEARNING SYSTEM

ut none of the magic

Video

The Mastery Videotape Series features fly fishing authorities who pass along a lifetime of knowledge. You can learn the principles and techniques that will help you be more successful whether you fish for trout, steelhead or tarpon. Everything from casting to reading the water to all the most important presentation methods. You can even learn how to tie the most effective fly patterns.

Six of our videotapes are also available in a Mastery Learning System set. Each set includes a Mastery videotape and a hardbound companion book that contains "step-by-step" explanations and detailed illustrations of various fly fishing techniques. These books direct your attention to the most important concepts in the videotapes and teach you to see with "expert" eyes. You'll also find specific terms, diagrams and definitions that will provide you with a wealth of knowledge. The guidebooks and videotapes work together to help you learn faster than any other method. Simple, easy to understand instructions directly parallel what's shown on the video.

Whatever videotapes you select, you'll play them over and over as you master the information and skills they present. Because they use them repeatedly, fly fishers are now building their own video libraries, adding individual videotapes as their fishing interests grow.

Introductory

Fly Fishing Magic

More and more anglers are finding that fly fishing is not just a great way to fish for trout. It's an exciting and effective way to catch a wide variety of fish. This videotape captures the thrills, enjoyment and beauty of fly fishing in all its forms: bluegills, trout, large-mouth bass, steelhead, bonefish, tarpon and more!

Fly Fishing Made Easy

You'll learn to enjoy this sport of fly fishing faster than you ever thought possible. Whether you're after bass, trout or panfish, your fly fishing instructor, Bob Guard, prepares you with these easy steps: **select a balanced system** of equipment for whatever fishing you choose; **assemble your system** the right way, the first time; present your fly to the fish with **basic casting** techniques.

You'll also get an introduction to the Scientific Anglers "Formula for Success" that will help you catch fish in almost any situation. **Location**. By learning the basics of fish behavior and their feeding habits, you'll be able to locate your favorite species wherever you fish. **Behavior**. By understanding feeding habits and how best to imitate that food, you'll be able to choose the right flies. **Presentation**. By learning the basic casting techniques, you'll be able to make effective presentations of whatever flies you use.

This is the videotape that will teach you all the basics of fly fishing without any frustration. You can progress, step-by-step, at your own pace and develop a solid foundation that will prepare you to travel down the road to fly fishing mastery.

Formula for Success: Trout

Three of fly fishing's leading experts, Gary Borger, Doug Swisher and Rick Haefle, teach you how to consistently catch more trout and bigger trout even under the most difficult conditions.

They'll show you how to use the Scientific Anglers Formula for Success to locate trout, to identify what they're feeding on and how to best imitate that food. Then, they'll show you how to become a great caster and make effective presentations in any situation or condition.

This video will take you beyond the basics of the Formula for Success and show you how to apply the Formula to fishing for trout. By focusing on one species, you'll begin to build a base of special knowledge that's needed to have consistent angling success when fishing for trout.

Casting

Basic Fly Casting

The first hurdle to overcome in becoming a master trout angler is developing a solid foundation of casting ability. Doug Swisher shows you how to develop your casting skill through his uniquely easy-to-learn technique. You'll learn: why casting works, how to train your mind and muscles to make smooth, controlled casts, how to perfect the basic casting stroke, the principle of loop control, how to make straight line casts and shoot line for distance, the slack line cast and how to recognize your casting mistakes and correct them. The fastest way to learn fly casting, these methods will eliminate frustration and let you spend your time catching fish.

Available in a Mastery Learning System Set (with hardbound guidebook)

Advanced Fly Casting

Doug Swisher shows the experienced caster how to fish the "impossible" places and help you make the transition from good caster to master fly fisher.

He reviews the basic principles of casting, shows you advanced techniques for getting longer drag-free drifts, increases the accuracy of your slack line casts, teaches you to make accurate curve casts, demonstrates how to "fish the clock," so you can make drag-free presentations to every angle without changing position and how to increase your casting distance range with the double haul cast. With these skills, you'll have the ability to fish effectively in every fishing situation.

There's no contest. This is the one videotape that will have the greatest impact on your fly fishing success. Whatever the level of your presentation skills, you will learn many techniques that will improve them and help you get your fly in places you thought we impossible to reach. With the kind of successes you'll have after watching this video, you'll find yourself playing it over and over again to learn new things that will accelerate your presentation skills.

Available in a Mastery Learning System Set (with hardbound guidebook)

Trout

Anatomy of a Trout Stream

Aquatic biologist and author, Rick Haefle, will show you how to find trout. He'll demonstrate how to read the water and to respond as conditions change. Learn to dissect a stream from end to end. Understand the basic needs of the trout and where to find them. Recognize the important food in all types of water. Become adept at selecting the proper fly and presenting it to imitate the natural's behavior. With this knowledge, you can plan your strategy to fish any piece of water and consistently catch more and bigger trout.

Available in a Mastery Learning System Set (with hardbound guidebook)

Fly Fishing for Trout

Internationally-known angling authority, Gary Borger demonstrates proven techniques for fishing dry flies, nymphs and streamers while fishing famous western rivers. An on-the-stream course in successful trout fishing strategies.

Fishing the Dry Fly

You'll see Gary Borger's special dry fly techniques at work on the difficult fish of Armstrong's Spring Creek, the Madison River and the Henry's Fork of the Snake and learn how to hook trout on your favorite stream. Gary covers strategies for fishing riffles, rapids, flat water and still water, including an exciting demonstration of his "secrets of the Henry's Fork." This video will teach you versatility so you can fish these different water types with a dry fly. You'll be able to read the water, select the proper fly and make effective presentations.

Available in a Mastery Learning System Set (with hardbound guidebook)

Strategies for Selective Trout

Author Doug Swisher shows you how to make the evolutions from a capable angler to a master fly fisher. By combining your physical casting skills with the mental skills of knowing what strategies to use during hatch and no-hatch situations, you'll be able to catch selective trout when others can't. Let Doug show you: how trout select their food and how you can imitate it; his strategies for fishing a typical hatch from bottom to top and how to make super long drag-free presentations for any position.

A complete formula for success for catching even the most selective trout.

Available in a Mastery Learning System Set (with hardbound guidebook)

Advanced Strategies for Selective Trout

This videotape will show you how to reach the highest plateau of angling mastery. Doug refines the techniques of "Strategies for Selective Trout," shows you how to master specialized techniques for no hatch situations like streamer fishing and cover more water in less time. You'll also learn how to stack mend for the ultimate deep nymphing fishing, learn to tell what trout are feeding on during multiple hatch periods and fine-tune your presentation skills to catch trout when they're midging.

Available in a Mastery Learning System Set (with hardbound guidebook)

The Way of the Trout and Fly Fishing the English Way

These two videotapes will give you some special perspectives on trout fishing. The first video, *The Way of the Trout*, presents a unique underwater view of the entire life cycle of the trout—from tiny fry to successful predator—that will give you valuable insight into trout location, feeding and behavior. A classic film with some of the most exceptional photography of trout ever filmed. *Fly Fishing the English Way* takes you overseas to the birthplace of fly fishing and lets you see how modern English anglers approach the sport. Special emphasis on stillwater fishing and the most successful techniques.

Steelhead

These four videos of the ultimate West Coast fly fishing challenge, catching steelhead on the fly, feature noted steelheading authorities, Lani Waller, in three videotapes and Jim Teeny in a fourth. Even though you may have fished extensively for rainbow trout, steelhead are a whole different breed.

You'll need to use totally different tackle and angling techniques to successfully fish for steelhead. These are big fish. Most anglers are a little stunned when they discover their size and power. When they hook one of these bruisers that are in the 10-15 pound range but can run over 20, they find out in a hurry if they've got the right tackle!

If you want to get serious about steelhead—particularly if you're going to take a Big Trip—this series on steelhead is great insurance to assure you of success.

Fly Fishing for Pacific Steelhead demonstrates all the fundamental concepts

and techniques you'll need to enjoy consistent angling success for these magnificent fish. Steelhead behavior, where and why they hold in different parts of the river, what tackle to use and how to present your fly.

Advanced Fly Fishing for Pacific Steelhead

Builds on the fundamentals of the first videotape and teaches you the skills you'll need to catch steelhead under the most challenging of situations. You'll learn about the things that influence steelhead behavior, proven methods for finding and hooking fish in deep water and how to fish the classic steelhead presentation methods.

Fly Fishing for Trophy Steelhead

Takes you on an adventure to the wilds of British Columbia in pursuit of trophy steelhead. Lani demonstrates his favorite dry-fly techniques, how to approach each new piece of water with a specific plan, how to adapt classic steelhead presentation methods to trophy situations and how to handle 20-pound steelhead in heavy water.

Catching More Steelhead

Fishing to sighted fish is the ultimate thrill in fly fishing for steelhead and the cornerstone of Jim Teeny's highly effective, exciting and unusual methods. You'll learn his unique techniques for spotting, stalking and

hooking steelhead under the most challenging situations. You'll also learn how to effectively "time the run" and choose a river plus select the best equipment to make the proper presentation. These techniques will work for you wherever you fish for steelhead.

Tarpon

The ultimate fly fishing experience.

Whether you've already had your first tarpon encounter or are still in the dreaming-about-it-stage, these two videotapes are made for you. Featuring tarpon world-record holder, Billy Pate, who shares his knowledge learned from hooking over 4,000 tarpon, these tapes are your shortcut to becoming a knowledgeable tarpon angler fast. These videos will help you avoid the "culture shock" many anglers experience when they hook up with their first tarpon and the problems they have tangling with one of these brutes.

Fly Rodding for Tarpon

Shows you how to spot tarpon, exactly what tackle you'll need and the casting techniques necessary to hook up with these silver kings of the salt. You'll learn where and when to cast and see which fly patterns and retrieves will consistently produce hook-ups. You'll then be guided through the skills you must have and the strategies you must know to land one of these super-charged fighting fish.

The Challenge of Giant Tarpon

Builds on the principles and techniques demonstrated in the first videotape. Billy shows you how to make the transition from landing average weight tarpon to fighting "box car" size silver kings. If you've ever dreamed what it's like to tangle with one of these huge fish weighing nearly 200 pounds, this is an exciting way to feel each strike and share in the thrill of every jump.

Fly Tying

There is nothing more satisfying than taking fish on flies you tied yourself. Our Mastery Series of three tapes—*Tying Trout Flies, Tying Hatch Simulator Flies* and*Tying Attractor Flies*—will teach you all you need to start tying flies that will take your favorite species. Master Fly Tyers, Gary Borger and Doug Swisher, will take you step-by-step from the basics to the more advanced techniques you'll need to tie 90 percent of all dry flies, nymphs, streamers and Doug's special patterns. How to select and use tying tools, materials, hooks to get started and, with practice, tie your own creations.

NOTES